Fro..

Also available from Cassell

Barnard *Cross-cultural Communication*
Barsoux *Funny Business*
Hayes *Systematic Networking*
Mallinson *Public Lies and Private Truths*
Moore *An Invitation to Public Relations*

French Resistance

Individuals versus the Company
in French Corporate Life

Michael Johnson

with illustrations by the author

CASSELL

Cassell
Wellington House
125 Strand
London WC2R 0BB

127 West 24th Street
New York
NY 10011

British Library Cataloguing-in-Publication Data
A catalogue record for this book is available from the British Library

First published 1996

ISBN   0-304-33911-3 (hardback)
           0-304-33912-1 (paperback)

Typeset by Stephen Wright, the Rainwater Consultancy, Longworth, Oxfordshire

Printed and bound in Great Britain by Redwood Books, Trowbridge, Wilts

Contents

Preface

It would be sad indeed to contemplate a France completely transformed – a France homogenized, conformist, and integrated with the rest of the world. Isn't the foreigner's love affair with France all about her iconoclasm, her bloody-mindedness? Nobody wants France to become more like us.

But change is in the air. During the strikes at the end of 1995, Prime Minister Alain Juppé said it clearly: 'France is at a crossroads. Its only choice is between change and decline.' The great sweeping trends in international business, in the name of ever-increasing economies of scale, are forcing change upon all countries, including France. Foreign economists and political leaders are rushing to embrace the new world order.

True to form, France is a most unwilling partner, irrespective of Monsieur Juppé's brave words. Change means overturning tradition, and France is the Western World's ultimate land of ritual, the land of the correct way of doing things. The Chinese are said to be drawn to the French because both cultures have elaborate traditions in two areas that matter so much to them: personal behaviour and cuisine.

Many French, like the Chinese, have decided over centuries that their rituals, including work rituals, are correct, and therefore radical change is not and will never be necessary. There is little doubt that disruptions and national strikes will be mounted to block change, and that the population will eagerly man the barricades. Although a minority seems prepared to consider change, that matters little in French-style democracy. Violent street demonstrations are part of the culture, and they have a way of achieving their goals. How long before the mood is tipped in favour of change? One generation? Two? Many more years of crisis will be required to make an impression on the *résistants*.

Of course not everyone in France is committed to worshipping the past. A minority voice is heard with increasing clarity, arguing from facts and reason. But this book is about the core of the country, the holdouts in France, employers and employees who cling to comfortable traditions, who reject the Anglo-Saxon notion that change is natural. In France, to deny the harsh economic realities of the modern world is a way of flaunting one's individuality, crying out Tarzan-like to tell the jungle of global business to go to hell.

This book is a portrait, viewed through the eyes of a foreigner, of the individual versus the company, a struggle in which at the current pace there will be no winner for many years to come.

If Britain is a nation of shopkeepers, France is a nation of talkers. The problem for France is that of being caught in circular debates. The thinking and talking in France today are so conditioned by the past that new ideas in politics and economics are rarely heard. Except for a brief fling with socialism in the 1980s, the country has been in the thrall of big, paternalistic government, yesterday's ideas, and the same *élite* managerial class for more than 30 years.

The stranglehold of the past means that new players, and the progressive solutions they might contribute, are unable to emerge into positions of leadership. Meanwhile, the rest of the world is moving forward to cope with the new realities of the global economy. The single market in Europe and the globalization of business are but two potent forces wrenching aside barriers in other countries.

A study by the Heritage Foundation in Washington argues that economic freedom correlates directly with prosperity. France ranks only eighteenth on the Foundation's list of free, prosperous countries, the lowest of Europe's developed countries and behind Estonia and Ireland. One unfortunate consequence of the failure of dynamism is the country's unemployment rate, the worst of developed Europe.

The suffocation of new ideas in France extends to the way companies are managed. While some firms have tried and succeeded in their modernization of work practices, many more have resisted. Modern management techniques – empowerment, teamwork, organized quality management – go against the grain of the traditional French mentality, and the employees are having none of it.

Accountability is not the Frenchman's idea of a better work life. The French view of company goals is defined by a strong individualistic culture that limits personal commitment to the concept of a company. Sparks fly when the Latin temperament of the French collides with the alien Anglo-Saxon business environment creeping catlike into the country as part of the internationalization of business.

Comparing and contrasting French work life with that in Britain and the United States, I was not always sure about the rights and wrongs of the situation. I caught myself many times wondering if the French hadn't perhaps avoided some of the traps we fell into, our mania for more and faster and better work at the same or less compensation. At what point does work begin to detract from rather than add to our quality of life? At 10 hours a day? At 12 hours a day? This is a question the Anglo-Saxon world prefers to avoid. But the Anglo-Saxons show no sign of slowing down. Recent studies show that workers in the US put in the equivalent of two months a year more hours than the French worker. And the US university graduate is now working more than 55 hours a week, ever more willing to assume responsibility as a way of proving his or her talents.

The Frenchman asks, in effect: 'To whom does it make sense to push authority and accountability down to lower and lower levels?' To management, of course. 'Who benefits from my increased burden?' Management, of course. 'Where is the speed-up leading?' It allows you to keep your job, if management so wills. From this perspective, the traditional French worker may be the first to have understood some of the aims of modern management.

It was Max Weber who nearly one hundred years ago drew the line separating Europe into two great regions – the Protestant north, with a strong work ethic, and the Catholic or Latin south, with a lesser commitment to things like work and its presumed reward. France has traditionally sat on the Catholic/Latin side of the line. Some French intellectuals want their country to migrate to the north zone, in effect to join the mentality of the Germans, the Dutch and the Scandinavians. In consumer expectations, economists say, this is beginning to happen. But others, in significant numbers, want to stay where they are.

The complex French people, so witty, so stylish and so hard to know, will have to change eventually in order to share in the prosperity of the developed world. They have much to lose as the economic pressures of a new and more open economic system begin to squeeze them. The Old France will one day have to give way, if only grudgingly, to the influences of the global economy.

In France, the 15-member European single market is having little effect today. The riots at the end of 1995 were about economic reform leading up to economic convergence with Germany and European Monetary Union (EMU) by 1999. The *Economist* magazine published the most telling picture of the turmoil, Parisian barricades in flames, headlined: 'France prepares for EMU'.

In 20 years we may look back and find that the pace of change accelerated as younger generations supplanted the Old Guard running business and government at the end of the century. In the next millennium, France will probably be a very different place, but will it be improved? And for whom?

Michael Johnson
August 1996
London

Acknowledgements

This book sums up a lifetime of involvement with France. Of course every French person I have known contributed in some way to the final product. But those who helped me sort out the differences include first of all my wife, Jacqueline, whose keen eye misses nothing. Next, it was my former colleagues in publishing, notably the woman who gave me the opportunity to work in a purely French environment, Anne-Marie Finkelstein. Others who pointed out differences, and read or commented on parts of the manuscript, included Yannick LeGoff, Virginie Robert, Daniele Lejais, Pierre Lombard, Pierre Vandeginste, Pascal Maupas, Anne-Marie Roussel, Stephanie Bonnet, Maurice Bood, Kenneth Dreyfack, Leigh Bruce, Stan Macklan, former *Management Today* editor Tom Lloyd, cross-cultural specialists and fellow-francophiles Polly Platt, Aviva Wittenberg-Cox and Ann Bengtsson, academics Peter Lawrence, Jean-Louis Barsoux, Jay Szarka and Robert Moran, and psychologist Paul Thorne.

Introduction

'Each society is a case of multiple personality, and it modulates without a qualm, without even being aware of what it is up to, from Jekyll to Hyde, from the scientist to the magician, from the hard-headed man of affairs to the village idiot.'

Aldous Huxley

France is a confounding country, even to the French. I blame the confusion on its stormy cultural history, a violent journey of domination and submission, glory and shame, ups and downs, ins and outs, rounds and rounds, that unintentionally has produced a schizoid nation. To outsiders, it seems that two, sometimes three, personalities can live happily within the body of a single Frenchman. For example:

- The French are trained to think within the hard confines of Cartesian logic but they revel in their Latin emotions. Try listening to their sentimental popular music.

- They have a sense of grandeur that puts the rest of Europe to shame, but small-mindedness is pervasive in everyday life. Try arguing with a shopkeeper.

- They are modern, high-tech and forward-looking, yet their manners and morals are *très dix-neuvième*, as they call their many vestiges of the nineteenth century. Watch them at dinner parties.

- They are jingoistically 'Franco-centric', but they are fascinated by foreign leaders and world events. In the space of one month, the presidents of China and the Philippines and the Emperor of Japan were grandly welcomed to Paris. Only Washington is so popular among the statesmen.

- With De Gaulle gone, they have lost their place in the world of global politics, but they are able to dwell blissfully on their more glorious past. Nicolas Chauvin, the Napoleonic foot-soldier for whom the 'ism' was named, was of course a Frenchman.

These beguiling people, with all their inner contradictions, are capable of enlightenment and darkness on an equally grand scale. All of this makes for a sweet and sour psychological soup, not to everyone's taste.

Study by total immersion

There is no better way to study another culture than to marry into it and to try to make a living on the local economy. I have done both. My 30 years of marriage won't be of much interest to anyone, but the lessons I learned from my career in the French business world may be instructive to others who attempt to cross over.

After departing from Paris in 1992, I set about capturing on paper my unusual experience. This book is the result: the story of my attempts to understand the French by living inside their society, working there and making a professional life on their terms. In France as in any culture, many themes intermingle, some pleasant, some not. My story concentrates on barriers and problems rather than on the warm and fuzzy memories that were also part of the experience. For it is the problems that fascinate, that force adjustment and that educate. It is the problems that we must turn over and over in our minds, to find the explanations, to see the logic.

I had a rare chance to live and breathe the French world of work first-hand, and I was at once excited and disappointed by what I saw. I drew upon my previous 30 years of international experience to grasp what was happening.

Cultural blindness

The real France took me by surprise. With hindsight, I can see that my confusion was due in part to my own cultural conditioning. I had never seen so many conflicting forces co-exist within a national neurosis. Most difficult for an Anglo-Saxon to accept was the fact that France was more than a haven for rigid logic – although there was much of that about. It was also a mystical (we now say spiritual) place where intelligent people have a lot of time for graphology, the alignment of the planets, and an attitude that they cheerfully call '*l'irrationnel*'.

Being happy in France is all about unlearning – casting off of old habits and old thinking, and replacing them with what works inside France. Indeed, unlearning our native cultural reflexes is the first step toward becoming an internationalist – accepting that other national patterns of thinking and behaviour have their own legitimacy. The foreigner must learn to enter that new world with mind and eyes open. It is not as easy or as amusing as it sounds.

Understanding foreign cultures is difficult because we all tend to look at others through our own distorting prism. Most foreigners are brought up to believe their home culture is the ultimate. I was struck by an inflated slogan in France: '*Impossible n'est pas français*'.

Americans are perhaps the most shameless in assuming superior national airs, but they are not alone. 'Rule Britannia' can still stir a down-at-the-heel British crowd, although it sounds slightly ridiculous to non-British observers. The Danes like to remind the Germans of the old Danish domination of parts of their mainland, and they still needle the British over the triumph of Canute, the Dane who proclaimed himself King of England in 1016. The Germans and the Japanese have acted out their superiority complexes in this century. The Chinese symbol for their country actually means 'centre of the universe'. Even the poor Russians like to flex their egos. As they used to say while basking on the pebble beaches of the Black Sea, 'Everything is bigger in the Soviet Union – even the sand'. Of course now Ukraine and Georgia run the big Black Sea ports.

What's wrong with being French?

Pride in their glorious past has given the French self-assurance in their style of life, and they are not inclined to take lessons today from the Anglo-Saxon world. They have long since made up their minds that being French is quite a reasonable state of mind, perhaps the world's best. Working with the French, I gradually realized it was presumptuous of me to try to turn them into us. The way forward in France as in any cross-cultural business situation is not the imposition of alien ideas. It is the merging of selected national strengths from both sides. The result must combine the best elements of the old and new worlds without violating the host culture. The visitor, as outsider, will inevitably be forced to adapt more than the host.

It was only after my experience in France that I learned how much study of international cultural adaptation had already been done. The father of the discipline is Edward T. Hall. Another leading voice in the field is the Dutch sociologist Geert Hofstede, an ex-IBM human resources executive turned academic. Anyone who undertakes an international move can get a sense of the future by reading the works of Hall and Hofstede.

Hofstede lays out in great detail the adventure that the cultural transplant is likely to encounter. Whatever is happening to you, Hofstede has seen it before. He starts from the grim assumption that we join the world of foreigners ignorant of the rigid habits embedded in the new environment. He writes, 'In a way, the visitor in a foreign culture returns to the mental state of an infant, in which he or she has to learn the simplest things all over again. This usually leads to feelings of distress, of helplessness, and of hostility towards the new environment.'

Accepting the unknowable

I shall attempt in this book to bring some understanding to the mysterious world of French attitudes toward authority, office rituals, motivation and conduct in the workplace. Let us be modest, however, in the face of human behaviour. Studying motives on a national scale is like trying to make sense of the universe. The connections that seem to form a coherent picture often blur upon closer examination. Paradoxes, contradictions and unknowables abound. As in the sky at night, is Ursa Major a Great Bear, or do we just want it to be? Are the French naturally counter-suggestible, or is that just our mindless reaction to their different point of view?

When faced with these questions, it is worth pausing to find something better than an automatic reflex answer. Indeed, without a superhuman effort to unlearn, then relearn, we are all doomed to endless bouts of cross-cultural head-butting. Not that better answers spring forth easily. In a foreign society, a pattern may emerge but where are the distinct boundaries, where is the perimeter? At what point does a generalization about an entire nation become unfair, unkind or even untrue?

Yet I insist that national traits do exist and can be defined. Americans are recognized on the streets of Europe by their loud voices and their free-wheeling body language. Germans wear distinctive clothing and seem to take possession of their new habitat, whether a beach, a bench or a bar. Italians will knock you over or put out your eye with their flailing gestures.

One study of the French purports to have determined the US and French ways of walking: The American male tends to swing his shoulders and hips while churning his arms. The Frenchman tries to take up less space:

no sideways swinging; the leg is stretched far out in front, the foot hits heel-first, torso rigid, while the forearms and the head keep the forward movement going.

The defining touchstones

It was the French historian Fernand Braudel who wrote that a nation will recognize itself in 'a thousand touchstones, beliefs, ways of speech, excuses, in an unbounded subconscious, in the flowing together of many obscure currents, in a shared ideology, shared myths, shared fantasies'. The trick in a book like this is to capture today's ideologies, myths and so on, and to pin them accurately to the page.

Once on the scene in France, it didn't take me long to grasp certain differences. I immediately saw that dreaming about Paris and working there as a manager are two quite different things. I soon realized I had known only the France of the outsider – as a tourist and as a foreign business short-timer.

Inside the procedures changed. Prejudices, closed micro-societies, clubby connections based on origin, education or religion,[1] and distrust of outside notions blocked many new ideas, many of my efforts to change the work culture. In my experience, the famous mental combativeness of the French character turned to resistance, then finally bloody-mindedness.

Armchair anthropology

The complexity of French culture, like any other culture, is daunting. Strands and patterns are as tangled as the human spirit. This perhaps explains why many attempts to describe national cultures in a paragraph, a page or even a book seem so unsatisfactory – especially descriptions of our own. I once heard a Polish journalist declare that the key to understanding the British mentality is the concept of indifference – indifference to food, indifference to sex, and indifference to each other. It trips off the tongue nicely but is short on nuance.

Most studies of foreign cultures are based on second-hand

---

1 The French who came back from North Africa after Algerian independence have formed a Mafia of their own; the Jews understandably watch out for each other; the Protestants have formed a tight network.

investigations. Corporate anthropologists have developed a methodology for camping out in companies for a few weeks or picking out small groups that they judge to be representative. I call this kind of study armchair anthropology. Their insights are often interesting, while suffering however from an arm's-length feel. Even Hofstede's studies are based only on questionnaires filled out by IBMers, albeit 160,000 of them. Moreover, one could argue that IBM's culture is a world of its own, and therefore not much of a model for the rest of us.[2]

Joining the system

I spent five years in France as a foreign correspondent in the 1970s, then returned in 1990 to work for CEP Publications, Groupe Tests division, a very French publisher of books and trade magazines, based in Paris. The company is *'franco-française'*, or deeply, dogmatically French and proud of it. Internal critics of the company go a step further and call it *'franchouillard'*, a word that drips with sarcasm and means something like 'stubbornly, backwardly French'.

Much of my thinking on France is based on my work in this company, but I was also an attentive observer of society and the business culture around me while working there and during my earlier stay in France, when I reported on business and economics for *Business Week* and other McGraw-Hill publications.

This is a personal memoir. My observations and conclusions are unscientific. Whatever the opposing views, in any case there is no single path forward. Few rights and wrongs can be isolated in this field. Nor can I claim that my analysis is always applicable to the great mass of French companies. France is being forced to change, like all countries attempting to function in the global economy. Leading international brands such as Alcatel Alsthom, Groupe Thomson, L'Oréal, Cap Gemini Sogeti, Pechiney and Rhône Poulenc have replaced outmoded management practices with more international attitudes. Lesser companies in Paris and the provinces cling to their privileges on the local market, their cosy

---

2 The 'IBM way' is sufficiently evolved to have its own unofficial internal handbook of jargon, a dictionary of thousands of acronyms and business/technology terms peculiar to the IBM culture. It is a language that reflects the culture, just as French reflects France. To an outsider, many of the terms seem bizarre. For example, ideal investment plans are called WIBNIs for 'Wouldn't It Be Nice If . . .', and a questionable financial estimate is a PANOOTA for 'Pull A Number Out Of The Air.'

associations with clients and suppliers, protectionism and the internal personnel practices inherited from another era.

My experience turned out to be a murkier mixture than I anticipated: moments of great personal enrichment, flashes of understanding, considerable hilarity and some achievement – but with the pleasures too often nullified by terrible frustration and hard lessons.

Francophiles and other foreigners heading into France to work, live or visit will, I hope, be less frustrated after reading these pages. Perhaps they will take away something useful, and the French themselves might find the foreigner's perspective interesting, if perhaps twisted and irritating.

A modest objective

I have tried to sketch out the work rituals that I was able to observe in French companies today, and to place them in the context of the current specialist literature. I have not created a model for the future Europhile. I am only pointing the way around some of the obstacles I discovered.

When I arrived in France, I was an unashamed fan of the French, past and present, from Clovis to Chirac. By the time I left, my immersion in the culture had washed away most of my more naive notions, no doubt a healthy process. Today I am less infatuated with France, but more relaxed when inexplicable things happen. Even as I saw the flaws of the people and their ways up close, I was always grateful for the opportunity to study this fascinating animal called the Frenchman.

Part One
Learning to Love Hierarchy

1 The Perils of Cultural Cross-Dressing

'There is no point talking theoretically about the diversity
of France: you must see it with your own eyes, take in
the colors and smells, touch it with your own hands, eat
and drink it, to get its authentic flavor.'

Fernand Braudel

'What we commonly mean by "understand" coincides
with "simplify": without a profound simplification, the world
around us would be an infinite, undefined tangle that would
defy our ability to orientate ourselves and decide upon our
actions.'

Primo Levi

The first French people I met were elegantly formal Rotary Club travellers who were exploring the interior of the United States. They had just reached the poor state of West Virginia where I was working as a young reporter. I was assigned by my editor to interview them on their impressions of Appalachia.

The French visitors certainly stood out in the local crowds. They had the most extraordinary manners and, I seem to remember, great posture. Their physical intimacy intrigued me. I had never seen hand-kissing before except in movies. Nor had I seen men hug and kiss other men. I had never heard anyone actually say 'Oh la-la' except as a joke. And their remarks on some of the British and American sacred cows such as religion and alcohol seemed ever so worldly wise to me.

On their second morning in the American outback, as they gathered in the lobby of the Daniel Boone Hotel in Charleston, a man who ran a steel plant in Evreux was telling his fellow-travellers of his adventures the previous night. The group leaned forward, all ears, as the tall, suave gentleman related his story. His American host, a born-again Christian hillbilly, had roughly refused his bottle of fine cognac offered as thanks for a night's lodging.

'Monsieur was indignant. Monsieur told me: "This is not a drinking household,"' he recounted, attemping a backwoods twang with his French accent.

'Ooo la-la,' went the group.

'Monsieur told me to put the bottle back in my valise immediately, please, and not mention it again.'

'Ooo la-la,' the group moaned again.

'Not a drinking household? Could this be true?' the group wanted to know.

'Yes. This is going to be an arduous visit,' the gentleman predicted.

The French explorers thought they must have landed on another planet. They were learning for the first time that delicate, lovingly aged cognac can sometimes be considered an evil spirit. In the end, they cut a four-day stay to three, and fled to California.

Y'ALL JUST PUT THAT AWAY, PIERRE.
THIS IS NOT A DRINKING HOUSEHOLD!

Culture clash

The call of the beret

My only frame of reference for what I was witnessing in this French Rotary group was their local American Rotary brothers, who tend to be the exact opposite – simple toilers from the small-business community with minds to match, and best avoided when visiting rural America.

I was 21 and just escaping from the Midwest myself. I liked what I saw in the French. For a long time now, something in my genes had been making me yearn to wear a beret. I never told my Irish mother or my Scottish father, but I secretly wished I had been born French.

As far back as I can recall, France seemed to have it all – romance, creative energy, style, modern technology, food and girls. My travels to France in the 1960s and my first posting there as a foreign journalist in the 1970s confirmed my dreams. Speaking French came easily to me, and I loved the unconventional, stubborn French people I had come to know. How quaint they all were. And when they weren't quaint, they were sophisticated and clever, at least compared to Americans. In 1966, I married one, and have never ceased to learn from her.

My holidays in France over a thirty-year period were filled with warm, charming encounters with the provincials. Every new region I visited left me more intoxicated. The walnut liqueur of Brive-la-Gaillarde makes a fine *digestif*. The calvados of Normandy is my kind of apple juice. Nothing goes with *pâté de foie de canard* like a Bourgogne *rouge*.

Entering the workforce

I therefore expected effortless entry when I found an opportunity to move to France and join the culture as an equal. Just as in my dream, I would become a Frenchman. In 1990, I accepted an offer of a senior management job in a French company where I was to be the person who brought much-overdue change to the enterprise. The personal satisfaction of winning the job gave me a good feeling, and the prospect of carrying management illumination from the English-speaking world led me to expect quick success – because management our way was the most rational, most humane and most effective ever devised. I had been practising it and reading about it in the *Harvard Business Review* for years. I also had made a pretty good living by writing about it for several years as a business and management journalist. But as I settled into my French work routine, I

NOBODY'S TRANSFERRING
THIS GUY TO THE
RIVIERA !

Paris, centre of the universe

realized this was going to be no easy transfer of ideas. The French were distant, unresponsive and suspicious. I had never seen so many highly strung, unhappy people. Gradually, I began to understand part of the reason. France is a small place with power and prestige almost totally centralized in and around Paris. A career-minded French person has few options but to make a go of it in Paris. If the job turns sour, often there is no alternative but to put up with a sour life. Unlike other countries of similar or larger size, relocation to the provinces – to Bordeaux or Lille, Metz or Marseilles – is seen as professional withdrawal or plain failure.

Going abroad is impossible for most, because fluency in English is the only route to international mobility. France has no equivalent of the Anglo-Saxon corridor, which extends to such diverse climes as New York, Australia, California, the Philippines, and Britain. Even in Holland and

Scandinavia one can earn a living in English. The old French colonies are Third World basket cases. And to the puzzlement of foreigners, even Québec is considered an unattractive backwater.

Paris therefore becomes irresistible for a career-minded Frenchman. When I had worked in Paris in the 1970s, an angry French executive of a lift manufacturer came to my magazine's office to dump a dossier of secret, damaging files on his employer. He wanted me to write about his boss's misdeeds to get even for being transferred to Nice on the Riviera. When I tried to reason with him, to persuade him to accept this wonderful posting to the French California, he explained in that pure, French logic that Nice is no California – it is Siberia. Ergo, he could not endure the humiliation of being sent there.

He did what most of his fellow-Parisians would have done – he stayed in Paris in a lower-level job and endured the frustration. And no doubt he became difficult to work with. Self-esteem suffers, and the ego-bruised will often take out their unhappiness on colleagues, especially on their underlings. In multi-layered hierarchies, as in life itself, each level transmits unhappiness to the level below.

Bearing new management ideas

Still, I was willing to consider the French executive's stubbornness and other similar incidents as isolated aberrations. When I accepted the offer to move from London to Paris, I was optimistic. I was hoping to import some of the advanced ideas that had swept the English-speaking world of work over the past ten or fifteen years. At least I thought I could find a happy medium between the French way and what Anglo-Saxons believe is the enlightened British and American way.

Specifically, I wanted to soften the management practices of the company that had hired me. The company had been managed for years like most French firms, in top-down style, much like the military. But why wouldn't delegation and 'empowerment' work in France, or anywhere in the world? How could open-door management, walking-around management, fail to bring peace and compassion to the office? Aren't we all in this working life together? Wouldn't the French embrace a management style based on mutual trust? Aren't human drives the basic common denominator we all share around the world? And the ultimate truth: beneath our cultural conditioning, aren't we all the same, really? Answers to these questions nearly always turned out to be different from my expectations.

Confronting the challenge

Those first autumn days in Paris gave me mixed emotions. Outwardly, all seemed well. The ripe scent of falling leaves filled the air, I had enough money to eat anything, and, as Mark Twain once observed, even the children spoke excellent French. Most of my adult life I had hoped to be where I found myself – just a day away from starting to work in a French company. Now, at last, I had a chance to join the French on their own terms. I should have been celebrating, but I couldn't even work up an appetite. Despair was definitely not the emotion I wanted to be feeling.

I was alone in a dreary Holiday Inn on Place de la République, the nearest hotel to my new place of work. The lobby was full of Americans shouting across the room to each other. The help was sweaty and overworked. The air smelled of last week's air conditioning. The neighbourhood is what the French like to call *le vrai Paris*, but to me that evening it looked more like a crumbling, down-market slum.

My plan for the next day was to deliver an introductory speech in perfect French that would make my new staff love me and want to work hard for me. As I struggled to write it, and to feel good about it, I was also trying to soak up *le vrai Paris*. But the reality of my new life was fast coming into focus in that bare and charmless Holiday Inn bedroom. All I could summon up was a feeling of anxiety.

No mere expatriate

Immersion in the French way of life was about to put me in an unusual position. Most cultural cross-dressers are better equipped. Either they have a parent from the new culture or they work for an embassy or a foreign company that protects them from direct contact with the local system. One way or the other, they are partially cushioned from the culture shock. My case was different. I was beginning to realize I was like a circus performer on a tight wire and I couldn't see a net down below. Was I really up on a tight wire, or was I a clown? I spent a restless night trying to decide.

The truth is that most professional expatriates are content to toil away on the margins of foreign countries, nibbling at the corners of new languages and cultures. Diplomats, business people and international journalists abroad spend their lives observing the natives from the sidelines, like visitors to a safari park.

Americans are not the worst offenders. Culture-skimming is a phenomenon of our age. We can move so easily about the globe that we rarely slow down for a close look. Worse, most of us seem to have been taught from a young age to be suspicious of other cultures. For example, the British nurture a special loathing for the French, suspicious that the French might actually be doing something enjoyable that a Brit could never countenance. Is it the sex? The garlic? Frogs' legs on the dinner table? All that wine?

Taking France on the road

Meanwhile the French, like most cultures only more so, consider themselves a race apart. Living abroad, they congregate in their own ghettos, doing their best to carry France along in their baggage. One French executive who worked in Teheran through the Shah's downfall later could only talk about the great weather and the jewellery bargains. Some of the streets of South Kensington in London, near the French Lycée, are more Parisian than Londonian. In other countries it's the same story. North of New York, Larchmont is the suburb of choice for the families of French executives working in Manhattan. The school bus for the Manhattan Lycée makes a run through town every morning to pick up the assembled French children.

The French contempt for American ways is well-documented, although it seems more paternalistic than hostile. The cultural gap is glaringly obvious. Americans lack a grandiose history; they always will, and they don't care. But the French care a great deal. A Paris friend tells me he still feels cheated after paying two dollars to enter an American museum of 'prehistoric artifacts' somewhere in the Far West. Most of the exhibits were bones and arrowheads of American Indians from the early eighteenth century. This kind of thing strikes the French as hilarious. In France at that time, Louis XIV had installed his glittering court at Versailles, baroque music filled the air, and Voltaire was riding high.[1] Paris represented the apex of worldly refinement. Even today, the greatness of the seventeenth,

---

1 Even Voltaire had his faults. In an essay on the Americas, he told the civilized world of this big, unexplored continent where one finds 'swine with navels upon their backs, and men with dispositions quite different from ours'. He was half right.

eighteenth and nineteenth centuries are what keeps French pride alive.

I have known Frenchmen in New York who manage to go for weeks without speaking English or entering an American home. Many have never eaten a cheeseburger.

'I do not eat food with my bare hands,' a Parisian gentleman once said to me in horror.

He cut his Whopper into small pieces, finally managing to fork down half of it. The plague of fast-food outlets in France today may be changing some habits, but great strata of the French population still resist this particular American invasion.

Isolation – a global disease

Now the families of Japan's new managers are arriving in Europe by the hundreds. They don't like Whoppers either. 'Little Tokyo' in Düsseldorf, Europe's largest settlement of Japanese, is just like home, with sushi bars, restaurants, geishas, Japanese schools and sing-along karaoke bars. Locals who enter the favourite haunts of the Japanese abroad are eyed with anti-*gaijin* hostility.

In Brussels, the European Commission goes about its business with scarcely an acknowledgement of the existence of the host country, Belgium. Many Commission workers never meet Belgians except for shopkeepers and the taxi drivers who take them to and from the airport. The cab drivers have had to learn basic directional English to survive. Foreigners' nicknames for the hapless Belgians range from the extra-terrestrial 'Belgoids' to the dismissive 'Zhiques'.

But the more curious among the expatriates are frustrated by this outsider's perspective. They look for ways to push themselves to the limit, to cross the cultural boundaries, to live among the local flora and fauna. These were the noble thoughts that kept me from depression in the darkness and bare shelter of the Holiday Inn on the eve of the first day of my new life. I knew I was heading into unknown territory, but I was a pioneer of the new Europe, and I was trying to work myself up to savour the challenge.

It was late in 1990 and I had happily told my family to uproot once again. We had already lived in Moscow, New York and London. And once before, 15 years earlier, I had been posted to Paris as a writer for McGraw-Hill magazines. This time I was alone. My family was still in London attempting to sell our home. Ever the optimist, I proceeded to move on ahead of my wife and teenaged daughter to take up my senior management job in CEP, in a division called, for obscure historical reasons, Groupe Tests. The company publishes materials in French for the French market.

Cultures as tidy compartments

Like Alice in Wonderland, I had the sense of stepping through the looking-glass, saying goodbye to friends in London almost as if I were passing into a parallel universe.

The passage was indeed across a large gulf. It is quite amazing to see how little contact the ordinary, everyday citizen of the English-speaking world has or wants with the Continental peoples of Europe. I was correct in my suspicion that I would have to build a new life for myself in France. The surprise was that French life turned out to be even more fenced off than I imagined. Friends from my English-language past who tried to track me down in Paris usually gave up after losing two or three encounters with the company's French-only switchboard.

I thought I knew French, and I thought I knew France. With the new federal Europe trying to happen, I was eager to jump into the trend of cultural cross-fertilization. Unless I were being naive, international managers were in growing demand, and the future could only bring greater demand. Yet I knew I was taking a risk. If the projections were true, why didn't I see other managers making similar moves? Was this another management fad that existed only on the pages of magazines and business books?

I also wanted to believe that my 20-year career in international publishing would be useful to the insular French. In Paris media circles, the rich mixture of fact and opinion that passes for journalism was under scrutiny. The role model of the moment was a vague notion called 'Anglo-Saxon journalism' as practised by such newspapers as the *Financial Times*, the *International Herald Tribune* and the *Wall Street Journal Europe*. French trade publications were also behind the times in editorial technology and in international content. The company wanted me to show them how it's done. The whole idea sounded adventurous, as well as instructive, and it had every chance of turning out to be a perfect extension of my international career.

My task as editorial director was to apply rigorous Anglo-Saxon editorial techniques to *01 Informatique*, the leading weekly French magazine of the information technology industry, and three associated publications, while managing a staff of 55 French men and women.

First new skill – Gallic irony

My meeting on that first morning near Place de la République, just opposite the grand headquarters of the French Communist Party, gave me an inkling of what lay ahead. My boss, a provincial trade-journalist-made-good named Bernard, warned me which knives were out for whom, who was against my appointment and who were the two or three senior people likely to resign in protest.

'Don't let it worry you,' he said. 'This is normal.'

'Sounds like a typical happy family,' I told him, practising my Gallic irony.

I made a mental note that Bernard had not mentioned anyone being in favour of my arrival. In a separate chat, the human resources director, Bruno, had more advice for me. He suggested that in my first weeks I avoid using scare words such as 'change' or 'new'.

'Just say you want things to evolve,' he counselled. 'This will cause everyone a lot less worry.'

Whatever the euphemisms, working in a foreign company cannot fail to be a learning experience. The differences will be deep beyond all expectation, and the foreigner is obliged to understand and respect those differences. One of the few truisms in business is that change is unwelcome. Importing unfamiliar ideas from abroad into a place like France, a country that in many ways is frozen in time, is not likely to find quick favour.

As Jay Szarka of the University of Bath writes in his book *Business in France*, 'There is little point lending one's tailor-made suit to another person and laughing at its poor fit.' I would add that it is the foreigner who must clothe himself in the protective colouring of the new culture, much like an animal in the wild, to avoid destruction as an alien creature. I was learning to slow down.

My dominant impression in my first staff meeting was the lack of responsiveness. As I took in the assembled crowd, I saw long faces everywhere. The chill was not going away. What was I doing here? I knew only that psychologists and academics had written that it is the taste for something new that lures the people into sampling foreign cultures. What you find outside your own home work culture is usually more risky, but it is always less boring. Not an hour goes by without surprises, many of them good. And as in a marriage, the personal growth will often help bridge the natural ups and downs of daily existence. Those who study the mind of the internationalist say that the 'curiosity to learn' is a personality trait he or she carries through life. This must be me, I kept thinking as my future colleagues stared at me. If nothing else, I was heading for an educational experience.

From top-down to bottom-up

What interested me in France was the management culture, and this was a first taste. I had worked for eight years as a management writer, and knew that authoritarian ways in the workplace are frowned upon in most of the civilized world.

The new standard is bottom-up management, tapping the intelligence of all employees as a prime source of competitive advantage. It is the people on the front lines who understand the problems and know instinctively how to get around them. They should be consulted. This idea started in California and Japan, spread to the rest of Asia, to New York, then to London, and now was the subject of much pontificating in the inter-national business press. In my role as pioneer, I had chosen to be one of these agents of change in France. This was the chance of a lifetime to experience what so many other people, including myself, had been writing about for years – introducing change in an old-style company.

I had not bumbled into Paris entirely ill-informed. Like most visitors, I knew how to soak up the beauty. Even on the working level, the contrast of Paris with New York or London brings welcome relief. I immediately saw in my company that a more carefree attitude towards work replaces Anglo-Saxon earnestness, workaholism and greed. The more casual view of work may mess up a manager's productivity plans, but it can make sense from the employee's point of view.

I was gradually made to understand that the price of enjoying all the good things in French life was to be a complete transformation of my way of thinking.

2 Spotting Those Barriers to Change

'French society dreams of revolution but in fact is repelled by change.'

Michel Poniatowski

'The Frenchman is suspicious. Could I go so far as to say that he is born suspicious, grows up suspicious, marries suspicious, goes to work suspicious, and dies suspicious? I think I could.'

Pierre Daninos

Once settled in La Celle St. Cloud, just west of Paris, I plunged into the cultural gap I had chosen to explore. Several well-meaning friends loaded conflicting advice upon me.

'Praise them for everything they do well – watch for the good work,' one cross-cultural consultant urged. 'People crave approval in every culture.'

Another told me to stop worrying, that my own curiosity and affection for the country would shine through. A mischievous management consultant advised me to bluster in and change everything overnight, to shock the staff and get their attention. Another said the opposite: 'Softly, softly works best.' Still another predicted that the time was right: France was leading the way into a federated Europe, and every bit of cultural mixing could only be welcomed.

All of them were at least partly wrong. In French business as in France generally, the impediments to change are intimidating. Some of this resistance is human nature, regardless of cultural conditioning. But in France barriers tend to crop up more often – in relations between religions, between men and women, between young and old, between social and economic classes, between levels of education and training, between co-workers, between management and employees, between regions, between nationalities. Foreign managers entering French companies should be aware that they are likely to arrive unknowingly lumbered with several of these handicaps. And forcing change too fast will almost certainly bring the problems into play.

French business analysts have noted that the door is often closed to reform under the best of conditions. Such imported techniques as flat organizations, zero-defect programmes, computerization, quick and open e-mail communications and robotization have met with mixed results in France. Some workers have learned to be flexible, but others have revolted, feeling threatened or at best tolerating the change with a bad attitude: judging it as a necessary evil rather than an opportunity.

Meanwhile, US and British companies have worked hard at perfecting new concepts of teamwork, and generally found them to be sophisticated tools for bringing productivity gains, sometimes up to 40%. But even primitive teams in France can falter because the taste for groupwork just isn't there. However well-advised one is, however pro-French one starts out, it will be a shock to peel back the layers and take a look at the rigid work culture that lies beneath the surface. In an old-line company, what was quaint and curious on the outside often emerges as obstinate and resistant when viewed from the inside. In attitude, reporting lines and work habits, little seems to have evolved in a hundred years. Change does not come naturally in these circumstances.

Like some gloom-laden computer game, the barriers and bottomless pits loom at every turn. Even experienced Euromanagers, the hardened veterans of the international job circuit, are pulled up short by some of the contentious conduct in the workplace that can erupt when change is mooted. While Italy, Germany, Holland and other European countries have their cultural quirks, at least they have understood the economic gain that comes from pooling their intellectual resources. But trust is a requirement for such partnerships, including work partnerships, and trust does not come easily to the French. Relations with most colleagues are suspicious, wary, watchful. Relations between workers and management are the same only more so.

The missing link

Some measure of good faith must be present to create productive teams. Indeed, sharing of tasks cannot be gainfully undertaken without trust. A foreigner managing a French team will quickly yearn for this missing element as he tries to build a working machine.

As I established my weekly meeting routine, I began by talking of the value of teams and citing work well done. But a senior member of the staff sniffed to the group, 'He only wants to give us good news'. So much for the value of praise. Support from the top, I saw, was assumed by employees to be suspect. They seemed to be asking themselves, 'What might management want next, our souls?' I soon switched tactics, only to find that criticism went down even worse – raising hackles, and touching off defensive retorts. It was difficult to see where to turn next.

What makes the French worker tick is a unique set of values that contrast with those emerging in most of the industrialized world. A partial list of these differences illuminates the contrast. Each contrasting quality represents a barrier to the acceptance of imported techniques.

FRANCE	WORLD TRENDS
1 Job security is my right	Job security is dead
2 I will not leave Paris to find work	Mobility makes life interesting
3 Work is incidental to my real life	My work defines me, gives my life meaning
4 If I advance, I want guarantees	The more responsible the job, the less secure it will be
5 Responsibility co-opts my soul	Adding responsibility is self-realization
6 The team threatens my identity	Our team will get the best results
7 Job descriptions protect me	Job descriptions are starting points, not boundaries
8 Beware of new ideas	Anything is worth trying once
9 Management cannot be trusted	Management has a job to do
10 Profits enrich shareholders	If the company does well, I do well

Only by living there and working inside a French company, a truly *franco-française* enterprise, can these differences be witnessed and identified. In many of the traditional French companies, any attempt to import what might be called co-optive business cultures will be a discouraging adventure.

The schism in management culture

From the outside, it takes time to realize that the very concept of management in many French companies is different. The British or American manager sees his role as a coordinator of resources and activities. He judges it useless or even harmful to seem more competent than his subordinates in their own activities. Each member of the team is invited to contribute a separate skill or expertise, making the combination add up to more than 2 plus 2.

The French executive, in contrast, considers it important to have precise answers to any questions that subordinates might have about the work they are doing. 'Implicitly, he bases his authority more on a superior degree of knowledge and competence than on his talent for coordination and management,' says one academic study. The French manager does everything better. What he does best of all is to issue sharply defined orders that rarely require teamwork. The result, in a word, is centralization in France, and decentralization in the United States. The scene is thus set for basic misapprehensions.

The mistrust of Anglo-Saxons is acute. Anglo-Saxons have an ideological attachment to open market policies, self-reliance and profit. The French can accept some of these qualities but only if a prior company condition is met: a commitment to social responsibility. Resentment against perceived Anglo-Saxon attitudes takes hold when management seems to accept little or no responsibility for the fate of employees.

To work in France, this management principle must be accepted by the intruder: convert yourself to French mentality as quickly as possible, and only then begin to ease your way towards your alien goals. This is perhaps as it should be. The foreigner must assume the first burden of adjustment. Once accomplished, the barriers to communication may melt away to some degree.

To better prepare the way for surmounting the barriers between cultures, perhaps the foreigner's adjustment should begin with personal mannerisms. Some habits foreigners find difficult to shed:

- Americans in Paris must suppress their desire to slap backs or raise their voices in public.

- Male French managers in New York must control their urge to touch or kiss everything in a skirt.

- Germans in Parisian restaurants must learn not to link arms and burst into song after their second litre of lager.

- Foreigners in Japan should observe at least the basic conventions of the Orient: good manners, discreet behaviour, respect for others.[1]

The process of acculturation

Difficulties surmounting the cultural barriers should not be under-estimated. Management consultants call the process the acculturation curve. This is a learning curve that starts in the happy zone of 'euphoria' (usually the initial few weeks), then skids into 'culture shock' (a few bewildering months, possibly as much as a year), finally climbing out through 'acculturation' and into 'stability' (another year-and-a-half or two).

To work effectively in France, acculturation obliges the foreigner to cast off his old people-management methods and relearn new ones, to sharpen office politics skills, to rethink business ethics, and to set aside any hope of creating a team effort. The French business environment is everything they didn't teach you at business school.

Early in my tenure, the French government's computer company with the wonderful name of Groupe Bull fell to squabbling in public with the industry minister who was responsible for the hundreds of million dollars in annual subsidies needed to keep Bull afloat. The minister was saying, 'I run Bull'. The chairman was saying, 'No, I run Bull'. It looked like time for a reality check at Groupe Bull. At my weekly staff meeting I enthused over the opportunity this presented. Our reporting team would expose the nature of the fight, find out whether this was to be the last agony of Bull, and reveal whatever future plans for saving, merging or dissolving Bull were likely to be implemented. To achieve this considerable task in a week, I named a project coordinator and I asked everyone on the staff to contribute.'You have all been in this business a long time,' I reminded

---

1 There is always an exception. I once knew an American who had a long record of successful business in Japan dating back to the US Army occupation days of the 1940s. He never learned a word of Japanese. He addressed men by their first names. He demanded a sirloin steak in Tokyo restaurants, and a knife and fork with which to eat it. He had started his bad habits when the Japanese were on their knees economically and politically. He had achieved *éminence grise* status, and his hosts deferred to his loutish demands out of reverence for his age.

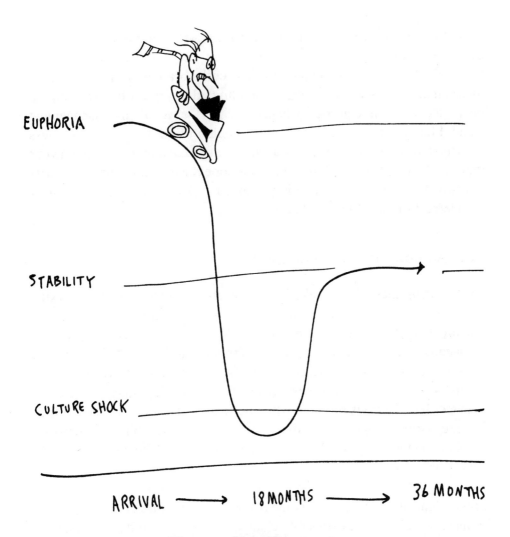

EUPHORIA

STABILITY

CULTURE SHOCK

ARRIVAL ———→ 18 MONTHS ———→ 36 MONTHS

The acculturation curve

them. 'You must all have friends and contacts inside Bull. Get on the phone.'

Another of the heavy silences I was getting used to then settled over the conference table. But I chirped on about the fun we were going to have getting to grips with this story. I then withdrew, and waited for the result.

When the research was completed a week later, I realized no one had grasped what I was talking about. Most of the story had been reported and written by the man assigned to coordinate it. A few crumbs were contributed by one or two others. The collaborative effort I had ordered simply did not happen. The concept of teamwork was alien to the culture.

Was there a lack of trust among these long-standing colleagues? Was each contributor holding back until certain he or she could somehow benefit? Was there a suspicion that collaborative work was anti-individualistic? I swallowed hard and admitted to myself that teaming up on projects was not going to happen with a wave of my management wand. I had been so far off target that I couldn't find the words to express my frustration. It was perhaps a mistake not to have legislated teamwork then and there. Or would that have made for even less collaborative spirit? For the first time, my French vocabulary failed me and we simply blundered further into the unknown

Handling cognitive dissonance

Experiencing these Teflon-like barriers against change can be perplexing to an outsider. The usual levers at a manager's command will trigger unexpected responses or no response at all. Psychologists and management consultants have a term for this, too. It is called cognitive dissonance – discomfort caused by beliefs, attitudes and behaviour so new that they seem to make no sense. If the dissonance dominates his life, the manager has a serious problem while he seeks a resolution of the conflict. To find harmony again, the novice must either put on blinders, head for home, or adapt his own behaviour. The third option is the only way for the serious internationalist.

The old Gaullist intellectual and writer Alain Peyrefitte understood the French fear of change, and his ideas matched up with my experience. In France, he believes, resistance to change has its roots in the reluctance to be compared unfavourably with other cultures. By rejecting new procedures, new techniques, one avoids being measured against other cultures. On the other hand, he notes, it is never good to oppose change openly. 'We prefer to say we want it.' He adds: 'The professions that end up getting dragged along with new trends despite themselves secretly hope for some divine intervention that will spare them'.

A key force slowing the change process in France is affection for traditional ideas – as if the great French Revolution (and Napoleon Bonaparte) said it all. A French friend who had always been at the top of the pyramid once asked me, 'What do you see wrong in our way of managing? It works. It has worked for a very long time. It gets results.'

This cultivated, highly-trained former CEO had never experienced the oppression of being at the bottom. It is perhaps not surprising, therefore, that he favours the status quo. And it is just as understandable that he sees the denaturing of the French way to allow a more homogenized international way of life as a threat to his identity. As in all human affairs, anyone who has a stake in the present arrangement will resist change. But in France, comfortable patterns of existence are so stubbornly entrenched that the ways of the outside world are perceived as only of marginal relevance. Nobody likes a cold shower, but in France, contentment in the warm bath of the present is particularly strong.

Proud to be French

The French in fact are, for deep cultural reasons, among the world's least exportable people. Although the rest of the world is moving about as never

WE FRENCH ARE VERY FULL OF OURSELVES — AND JUSTIFIABLY SO.

Strong national identity

before, my staff freely admitted that they prefer to stay at home where they have everything they will ever need. The depth of national pride is admirable, even among the young. A thirty-year-old colleague returning from a one-week trip to Washington told me, 'I am so happy to be back in beautiful France. After seeing America, I know how much I love my country.' He was still quaking from his encounter with a panhandler who had grabbed his sleeve and said: 'Gimme your change'. In Paris, the panhandlers have not yet started grabbing sleeves.

Common features with France's neighbouring cultures are in any case hard to find. Other languages are badly or rarely spoken. (France scores eighth out of twelve in language ability among her European Union partners.) Other cultures are viewed by the French as crude and crass, usually in terms of ancient stereotypes. For example:

- Italy is a third-world country wallowing in its own disorder.

- The Germans are vulgar and domineering.

- The British are vaguely admired but thought to be too peculiar to be taken seriously and too devious to trust.[2]

- The Belgians. Ah yes, the Belgians. They are in a class by themselves. It is only a slight exaggeration to say they are considered subhuman. A French friend of mine who has the misfortune to bear a surname with 'Van' as its first three letters always explains, a bit too quickly, that his family came from 100 metres inside the Franco-Belgian border. The prejudice runs deep, as he knows better than most. French drivers are conditioned to brake for cars with Belgian number plates. The Belgian behind the wheel is sure to do something sudden and brainless.[3] A statement that is simplistic and self-evident will be called 'Belgian'. Indeed, in designing magazine pages, editors will refer to the simple layout or plain-language headline as 'Belgian' – perhaps the worst kind of pejorative because it is not a joke in this usage, it is used as a legitimate metaphor.

---

2 A study of negotiators who set up the Channel Tunnel project found that the French had this, among other things, to say about the British: 'The British negotiator weaves a subtle, invisible web around negotiations. Sly manoeuvres are often concealed behind their courteous, smooth attitude.'
3 The statistics perhaps justify the fear. Belgians have about 15 accidents per 1,000 cars annually, compared to about 6 per 1,000 in France.

- The Swiss are stingy and obsessed with foreigners, germs and regulations. ('Most things are forbidden. And what is not forbidden is mandatory.')

- Except for their aristocrats, the Spanish and Portuguese are best reserved for domestic help.

Cocooning inside the hexagon

Experts at barrier-creation, the French seem to be cutting themselves off wilfully from the outside world. Britain does the same, but at least has the excuse of its island geography. Americans are worse, but their economic self-sufficiency is a defensible explanation. Among continental Europeans, the French seem more determined than most to preserve their ways.

Yet in the French land of contrasts, in this land of contradictions and ambiguities, a certain worldliness coexists with the xenophobia. It is as if they want the doors to be closed, but the windows left open. Jean-Marie Le Pen can whip up a great froth of emotion in a crowd at the mere mention of North African immigrants, but the French media devote far more newspaper space and air time to foreign affairs than the US or British media.

At bottom, however, my experience taught me that Chauvin still rules. The few valiant voices in favour of open markets are usually drowned out by cries for more protectionism, more barriers. Incursions by foreign competitors are ignored as long as possible, then resented and denounced while being resisted. As France Telecom moves slowly towards partial privatization, fears of the future emerge daily. A labour leader spluttered to the press that he had discovered what the net result of structural changes would be: '*C–c-c-ompetition!*'

The French car industry is the most determined of all Europeans to block the Japanese from the new Single Market. Even in the international worlds of publishing and computers, the top managers of French companies tend not to speak the lingua franca, which happens to be English first and German a fast-advancing second. Protectionism, visible and invisible, is widely practised in all manner of industries, from VCRs to transvestite prostitution. When the French police moved in to clamp down on car sex peddled by South American transvestites in the Bois de Boulogne, it wasn't so much the moral issue that rankled. The police commander summed up the national indignation: *'Ces filles ne sont même pas françaises!'* ('These girls are not even French!')

A touch of xenophobia

Foreign expansion is tentative and haphazard, often because of a defensive arrogance regarding potential foreign partners. In my business, these cultural barriers led to international deals being missed. Friends in one French company tell the story of their visit to New York a few years ago with their chairman to discuss a partnership with an American company. The French chairman, who spoke no English, was so ill at ease in the morning session that he cancelled lunch and did not turn up in the afternoon to continue the talks. He was having trouble accepting a less than paramount role in the negotiations, and he had just realized that such international deals more and more happen in English. It finally hit him. Either he had to learn English, or stick to the French market. He opted for the French market, and spent the afternoon on Fifth Avenue shopping for his wife. The deal never went forward.

Only by lowering barriers – overturning tradition and giving up some comfortable habits – could the French develop the more open outlook required to function in a global business system. What might this mean in real terms? It certainly would mean the dismantling of cosy associations, opening up of sacred national territory to foreign business invaders, fuller compliance with the unforgiving laws of economics, and all the personal trauma for vested interests implied therein. Except for a handful of giant multinationals, France seems not to want this kind of upheaval.

The bygone era of French national grandeur is very much in the mind of young and old. The school system dwells on the glorious past, and institutions seem happily frozen in time. The whole nation tends towards a weakness for *torse bombé* ('swelled chest', a mark of pride) posture. In a recent survey, 75% said the preservation of a clear-cut French national identity is a priority for them. A French colleague summed it up for me in one of those great, sweeping generalizations tinged with Gallic irony: *'Les Français sont très imbus d'eux-mêmes, et à juste titre.'* (We French are very full of ourselves, and justifiably so.')

3 The Big Standoff in the Workplace

'Far from being allied, private interests and the
common good are mutually exclusive in the natural
order of things.'
                                        Jean-Jacques Rousseau

To manage people in France, it is best to start by accepting the unpleasant reality of management-labour polarization. There is no point fighting this basic truth. In the traditional French company, employees have problems finding any common ground between their personal interests with those of the firm. Try consensus management, try quality circles, try Japanese-style *nemawashi* (cultivation of the roots, as in *bonsai* gardening), try acting like a human being. You will be tripped up at every turn. A heavy air of confrontation impedes any attempt at candid, open-minded communication between levels of the hierarchy. In this chapter we shall look at some of the attitudes of lower echelons.

For some reason, the French seem to expect and even relish head-on conflict. In all realms, from politics to the arts to shopkeeping, direct confrontation is a way of life. The differing aims of labour and management provide fertile ground for this seed. Some specialists trace the French attitude to the feudal system, where classes were fixed and privilege was hoarded at the top. In the feudal world, as in France today, there was no friendly collaboration between adjoining levels in the power structure.

Others attribute the French way to top-down military systems – a management chain perpetuated by one of the main schools for the power *élite*, the Ecole Polytechnique. Again, the military trains people to find friends at their own level, not among the generals and certainly not among the underlings. Whatever the origins, the lines of separation and therefore the points of conflict are clearly set and difficult to avoid.

Workers in France today will tell you with some pride that they can't help it – they have revolution in their genes. It is surprising how frequently the subject of The Revolution occurs in conversation. The events of 1789 are often trotted out as justification for various forms of contentious conduct. It is difficult to tell whether the revolutionary past is the chicken or the egg. Are the French really prisoners of their past, or do they just find 1789 a convenient excuse for venting their Latin emotions? Whether feudal, military or revolutionary, the result is the same: authority figures are feared by the workers, and the workers are scorned by the men and women in authority.

Pranksters at work

A kind of guerrilla-style mischief-making sometimes goes on in the background while a newcomer is trying to get settled. When I first arrived in Paris, my office was burgled twice within two months and my computer memory tampered with. Not everything was erased, only my file of 500 addresses and telephone numbers – 20 years of contacts. No physical property was removed, but my locked filing cabinet was ostentatiously prised open, leaving bent and scarred metal as a reminder. This was a first salvo. I left it unrepaired for two years as my private souvenir.

A few weeks after my burglary incident, an article on the computer industry in a national newspaper saying the 'threat to France will be of American nationality' was highlighted with pink marker and posted on the bulletin board over a photograph of me that someone had dug up. The story referred to IBM's interest in acquiring part of the French computer company Groupe Bull. This time, the famous French gift for irony was not lost on me.

The signs were becoming clear. I was stunned by these pranks. The signals were telling me that an undercurrent of resistance was at work. All of my management experience up to now had been outside of France in countries where the work atmosphere tended to be collaborative. Was all that experience irrelevant? Could I be that naive?

In most modern companies in the Anglo-Saxon world today, it is accepted wisdom that a central pillar of people management is the productive people-relationships up and down the pyramid. What more could employees want from a manager than straightforward, positive human relations? In other countries, open-plan offices are commonplace. Top managers with open doors – sometimes with *no* doors – make themselves readily available to all levels of the company. I was an admirer of John Young's 'control tower' when he was chairman of Hewlett Packard. From his perch, Young could see co-workers across the room and vice versa, and his door was open to any of the thousands of HP employees who wanted to talk.

The take without the give

In modern Anglo-Saxon companies, a managerial attitude of collaboration normally will be welcomed. Managers with a good human touch are usually effective, respected and accepted. Toughness obviously has its place when necessary, but a surface atmosphere of positive collaboration is appreciated by well-intentioned workers. It also leaves the manager and the employees feeling good about their work.

THIS COMPANY IS RUN BY IMBECILES, AND I REFUSE TO WORK FOR IMBECILES!

A love of confrontation

In France, however, it often turns out that '*la base*', as the lower levels like to call themselves, goes to great lengths to keep confrontation alive. Two European academics who studied French and American business found an interesting explanation:

> From the Latin angle, labour unions have difficulty considering cooperation with management: it is still viewed as an unacceptable collaboration from the point of view of the class struggle. On the Anglo-Saxon side, union activity seems less politicised and more corporatist.

The basic split between the two sides becomes evident in day-to-day incidents. It is hard to imagine some of my experiences in the more controlled, professional atmosphere of business relationships in London or New York. But in France, workers are isolated, and their behaviour reflects this separation from the company's interests. They especially like to talk back. For a foreigner, it is this yen for face-to-face confrontation that is so surprising.

Some memorable vignettes from my time in France:

- A colleague once cornered me alone in the corridor and made this remarkable accusation: 'We know what you're up to. You want to sack us all and bring in your friends to replace us. You won't get away with it, you know.'

- A new department head felt the sting of confrontation on her first day. One of her staff took an instant dislike to her, and refused to shake her outstretched hand or speak to her – a kind of declaration of war against her own boss. When the employee was satisfied she had made herself clear, she turned her back and stalked off. Eventually the department head resigned in frustration.

- One keyboard operator quit with a flourish: 'I have nothing against working, but this company is run by imbeciles, and I refuse to work for imbeciles,' he told me.

- One manager in another company, known for his toughness, was accused of causing an employee's death when a recently dismissed worker committed suicide. The manager, who thought he had just been doing *his* job, stoically sat out the protest until it ran out of steam. For years afterwards, however, his ex-employees liked to whisper that he was responsible for a man's death.

Benefits: the national sport

Even the threat of dismissal has lost its meaning. A departing employee who had been sacked told me how pleased he was to be heading out the door. 'This is better than working,' he said. The young man, barely 30, knew whereof he spoke. Unemployment benefits are high, and peer pressure to find work is minimal. Many French, including the young, ask themselves, 'Why work at all?'

Being unemployed was a disgrace as recently as 20 years ago when jobless rate was running at 2%. The French believed they would maintain that low number forever. When the numbers started to climb in the mid-1970s, one nervous banker friend confided to me that he feared another revolution. He could not have been more wrong. One of the most fundamental changes in France in the past two decades has been the new attitudes toward employment.

Unemployment now being such a persistent feature of French life (14%, the highest of the developed European countries), joblessness carries little if any stigma. At worst, the out-of-work individual is considered an unfortunate victim. At best, he is admired for successfully getting his share of state unemployment benefits, and the state is considered to deserve a good purloining. While part of the French attitude holds the state responsible for protecting the people's welfare, another part despises the state for being so generous.

There is a general feeling that the high cost of welfare is justified by the relatively peaceful streets it helps ensure. Homelessness is a rising problem, but poverty and crime are less evident than in other major capitals, probably because more people in Paris have enough welfare money to survive in reasonable conditions. 'I consider it a tax against getting mugged on the streets of Paris,' a senior manager in another company once told me, 'and I am happy to pay it'.

The impact on initiative

Unfortunately the system is so easily abused that profiteering from it has become endemic, virtually a national sport. It is now evident that France can no longer afford to take care of its idle millions while also supporting the retired. Employers are paying between 43% and 72% on top of salary to keep welfare afloat. With 2.2 million people on welfare and another 3.3 million seeking their first jobs, the welfare house of cards has begun to collapse.

The welfare burden will have far-reaching effect as France tries to lower its budget deficit from more than 5% to 3%to meet European Union criteria for the single currency. One obvious solution is to cut back benefits and begin to live realistically within budget constraints. But this rational approach collided in late 1995 with the well-known French determination to cling to existing benefits, never accepting a step back- wards. Paralysing strikes happened then, and are sure to happen again as France attempts to fit its modern yet outmoded society into the grand visions of the twenty-first century.

French welfare, intended as a cushion, has had at least one unintended effect – snuffing out much of the initiative required to maintain companies' internal dynamism. Sackings of incompetent or superfluous employees are often more trouble and expense for the company than they are worth. From the worker's point of view, even if the worst happens, so what? Anyone on the dole can live quite comfortably for as much as two years. Indeed, some openly try to provoke their own dismissal by such methods as not showing up for work till noon, then disappearing for lunch till 4 pm. When the boom is lowered, they are delighted. They stand a good chance of coming out ahead. An employee who walks away with a good deal is often applauded by his comrades for having beaten the system. All he or she needs is for the termination to be classed as 'for economic reasons', and the worker is on his way. Often this will be quietly negotiated between employee and manager as a way of avoiding messy labour tribunals (*les Prud'hommes,* as the court is known in France). The employee then leaves for Spain or the Alps for a rest, after which he will return to Paris, see some movies, read the latest novels, do a little casual work, fulfil the minimum welfare system requirement for searching for a job, and quietly plan his return to the workforce just as his unemployment benefits run out. Meanwhile, the burden of supporting him has fallen on the taxpayer.

The tax burden too is putting a strain on the system. France now has one of the industrialized world's highest tax rates – 42% of gross domestic product, compared to 33% in Britain and 15% in Japan.

But getting one's share is the object of the game. Milking the welfare system is one of the classic *combines*, or sub-rosa deals, that the foreigner must understand and accept to be happy in France. One French friend advised me: 'You Anglo-Saxons will never understand French until you learn to accept the basic morality of *combines* as a way of getting through life.'

A health service with a heart

One of the *combines* that is widely accepted as harmless is the sudden illness. This is the favourite revenge of the worker who has been reprimanded. He or she rings in to report to the human resources department the following day around noon to announce that a doctor has advised two weeks of rest for nervous exhaustion. Doctors can easily be found to sign a sick-leave form on the flimsiest evidence. It is enough to complain that one is nervous and exhausted.

Of course not everyone is so inclined. In one of my departments, a hard-working woman limped in to work one day with her leg in a cast. She had literally tumbled down a flight of stairs the previous day chasing a story – trying to arrive on time for an interview. The same day, another journalist across the aisle from her decided to take three weeks off to recover from having an ingrown toenail removed. What puzzled me was that the contrasting behaviour of the two colleagues seemed perfectly acceptable to everyone else.

A painful crossroads

Promotion into the management team, on the rare occasions when this happens, can be a traumatic leap for a French employee from '*la base*'. Status and power tug in one direction, but a lifetime of labour–management polarization prevents easy mobility. My junior staff, far from seeking advancement, regularly told me how they pitied me, how they would never want to occupy my office, never want to move up the ladder. This kind of attitude seemed to stem from a fear of being bought off, or co-opted, by the forces of capitalism. An employee climbing the hierarchy is tortured by thoughts of betraying his comrades.

One of my managers had this problem. She could not seem to make what to her was a big choice – 'us or them'. She later confided to me the feeling of inner struggle she was experiencing. She was a manager, she acknowledged, but her heart would always be with '*la base*'.

Give and take

Choosing people is another minefield. A new manager in Britain or the United States loses no time identifying individuals suitable for responsibility. He is looking for people of competence, high energy level, an ability to accept constructive dialogue, accountability, and a willingness to make a commitment to the job. The employee knows instinctively when he is being favoured by a new manager, and he most likely responds with loyalty and a sense of satisfaction at being on the new team. Acting on past experience in his home country, a US or British manager will tend to plunge into the same process in France.

But, in France, life is not that simple. Employees *and* managers have problems establishing common ground. Interests of the two parties are considered mutually exclusive. The unwary foreigner who is too generous with his time and compassion will only confuse the employees. Chances are, the French worker has not seen such behaviour in an authority figure before. The motives of the manager will not be understood. The expected result – loyalty and commitment from members of the new team – will not automatically follow. The French employee, conditioned by a lifetime of distance from his superiors in all spheres, will hang back, believing that the less known about himself the longer he can safely hide in his cocoon.

The more friendly the manager becomes, the more the French employee will wonder where the booby-traps are, or, in the worst case, he will write off the foreigner as a hopeless softie. The manager is then left frustrated, having opened himself up to his future close associates, but with nothing to show in return. His openness will be interpreted as a weakness, not a strength.

Even that universal lubricant, money, is eyed suspiciously. I once gave generous bonuses to two of my management team who had just rushed a special project that required long hours and weekend work. In return, I expected at least a smile of contentment. Instead, in private meetings to hand out the largesse, one laughed aloud and said, 'Why? I didn't do anything special.' The other, whom I called in a few minutes later, said, 'Oh no, Michael. It's too much.' He was physically uncomfortable at the prospect of receiving what seemed like a favour from senior management. I thought for a moment he was going to refuse the bonus, but in the end, reason prevailed and he pocketed the cheque.

One executive of another French company who had worked in Britain for many years and recently returned to France told me how she confronted the hostile atmosphere in her office. She learned to gird herself for the worst possible petty confrontations before leaving home every morning.

'When fights erupted, as they nearly always did, I took it as normal behaviour. I wasn't caught off balance. And if there was no fight, I considered it a real bonus for the day and I went home feeling lucky,' she told me one day.

'How can you spend your life working like this?' I wanted to know.

'This is France,' she said. 'In our context it is normal.'

Counter-productive tension

The belligerent office mentality takes surprising forms in one-on-one meetings with employees. One woman who worked for me, known for her acid tongue, told me during a tough performance review what she thought.

'You are a liar. Everybody knows you constantly lie. It's the biggest joke of the staff. You have no idea what kind of trouble you are getting yourself into. This is going to be wonderful,' she said, laughing.

Was this a nightmare? I had to pinch myself. I had never even bent the truth, much less lied. I was supposed to fear 'trouble' from unproductive staff? Who was boss here? This would be a simple case of insubordination in most cultures, but in France, as I later discovered, follow-up action was not possible. There were no witnesses, so there was no case.

I was advised when I came on board in Paris that I was expected to become a father figure for the staff.

'They need a papa,' I was told.

'Fine,' I said. 'I like to think of them as a family anyway.'

'No, no. Be tough on them,' my superior corrected me. 'They want it that way.'

Like a good French papa, I was expected to beat them up at regular intervals. This imperious attitude was taken as the norm. One of the weaker staff members never had a chance. The question on the table at a senior management meeting was simple:

'*Est-il con ou est-il bête?*' ('Is he a jerk, or is he just stupid?')

'*Il est bête.*' ('He is stupid.')

'*Non, con. Sûrement con. C'est pire que bête.*' ('No, he's a jerk. Definitely a jerk. That's worse than being stupid.')

One wondered how with such handicaps he managed to get hired in the first place.

Young employees who speak their minds are sometimes labelled *soixante-huitards* ('68ers', referring to the students who rioted in 1968). Over-40s who speak their minds are known as 'retarded 68ers'. Managers are repeatedly asked to commit themselves on such off-hand judgements.

A starting point in these discussions 'whether or not staff cuts were coming' might be: 'Who are the three people you most want to get rid of?' The principle is that in any ranking of staff, there are always people at the bottom and they should be seen as candidates for the trash heap. After a year of housecleaning, I had trouble coming up with three more names.

Concentration of authority

Devolving authority at lower levels in a company – one of the most important trends in business throughout the industrialized world – goes against the grain in French management. As Sanche de Gramont (now rechristened Ted Morgan) wrote in his study of French behaviour, 'The habit of authoritarianism makes the French executive reluctant to delegate responsibilities; he spends an inordinate amount of time on police-like surveillance of his staff.' Since the students and workers won legal concessions in the riots of 1968, the system has loosened up considerably, but old habits are still there.

From the beginning, the struggle to manage effectively was very much uphill. The standard tools for encouraging professional growth – career planning, promotion up the hierarchy, salary increases, private or public praising of a job well done – had little effect. The 'soft' techniques and methods designed to let each individual blossom are not trusted.

We are not in this together

In theory, human nature is at its best in such free surroundings. But, in France, what is wanted is usually 'hard' techniques – imperious distance, harsh criticism, clear delineation of manager and managed.

Any effort by management to establish collaborative relations with the staff is viewed with suspicion. New ideas imported from America, such as the 'centrarchy', with an organization chart showing the manager not on top but in the middle, surrounded by employees like spokes on a wheel, would be treated as a joke in the typical French company. A friend in another firm in Paris told me what I didn't want to believe:

'They don't want you to be their pal. You must be cool and critical. Dominant and superior.'

The idea that we are all in the same boat, that we have common interests, that success would benefit us all, and that therefore we could actually enjoy working together, was too radical to consider.

After months of trying my best to get the French to break with their past, I abandoned hope of creating a positive collaborative atmosphere. I had used up all my ideas within a year or so – setting clear goals, working long hours, joining in the actual nuts-and-bolts work of each task, maintaining an open-door policy, roaming through the offices in the style of 'management by walking about' (MBWA), and that ultimate seducer that I had been advised would always work in France: taking them out to a good lunch one by one. The lower down a person in the hierarchy, the more trouble they have overcoming the deep-seated belief that management is out to exploit them.

For a foreigner, it was the world upside down. I took to explaining my ways by prefacing my explanations: 'On my planet, we find that it works to do things the following way . . .' While intended facetiously, it only confirmed their view that we were from different worlds.

4 The Missing Interface at the Top

'A gouverner les hommes de trop haut, on perd
l'habitude de les regarder.'

Maurice Druon

'They (the French) are doomed to be abstract.
Talking to them is like trying to have a relationship
with the letter x in algebra.'

DH Lawrence

In many French offices, it seems that imperious management attitudes contribute to the atmosphere of tension as much as does employees' rebelliousness. In the executive suite, top-down management is often the style of choice. Why? Frequently because the assumption is that the workers are blameless children. Many are considered unmotivated and possibly untrustworthy.

A climate of bitterness prevails in part because divisional managers, who suffer high-handed treatment from their own headquarters' executives, will typically replicate their superiors' behaviour in dealing with the lower levels in the company. Contempt for those who are smaller and weaker is a counterweight against one's own feelings of helplessness towards stronger individuals higher in the structure. In laymen's terms, they transmit the heat.

The fine practitioner of management theatrics will sometimes employ subtler means. A senior executive of my acquaintance somehow made it seem a privilege to be received in his office. It became an honour to enter the cavernous space, even to be verbally abused. The manager had not realized how overt his tactics had become until one of his more feisty junior executives arranged an appointment to resign. Upon entering the space, the young man taunted his soon-to-be ex-boss: 'I'm so pleased to be allowed in. What a nice office. I have always wondered where you worked. I have come to say I quit.'

Top management, it must be said, often seeks no dialogue. In one Paris-based company, a middle manager acquaintance of mine begged to differ when his superiors decided to reduce his tiny team from two persons to one. Concerned that he could not function with the reduced staff, he spoke his mind in a concise, reasoned memo that turned out to be a tactical mistake. His arguments were dismissed as a 'provocation', and a black mark was placed by his name. This man was labelled a troublemaker to be permanently sidelined. The staff reduction went ahead and he was forced out of the company.

In France, as in many other countries, the executive sometimes likes to heighten his aura of mystery by making himself inaccessible, almost invisible. One French manager of the old school enjoyed enhancing his prestige by overloading his schedule (he was *overbooké*, in the current franglais) so that he could keep two or three of his middle managers waiting in a queue, like patients in a doctor's office. Eventually he was brought down to earth by his superior, who asked him to cease his *anti-chambre* practice – a reference to the old habits of the *grand seigneur* in France who kept social inferiors waiting in his antechamber until he felt good and ready to receive them.

Lowering the barriers

Discussions between managers and the working staff of old-line French companies remind me of two opposing teams of lawyers trying their best not to communicate.[1] Every pronouncement is considered a provocation and *de facto* untrue. Both sides talk in legalisms to deflect possible retorts from the other side. Statements are turned inside out for inspection of their hidden meanings. As in the best legal discourse, whatever can be misconstrued will be.

Senior management, to avoid problems with employment law, communicates in tortured syntax. Simple memos on the air-conditioning system are stitched up in impenetrable lawyerly formulations. Not surprisingly, such management-speak raises hackles in the lower echelons. In response, notes from below are hammered out by committees that revel in the best belligerent trade union tradition – exaggeration of the problem, accusatory language, urgent demands – although actual union membership

---

1 Lawyers like to say, 'If you have the facts, argue facts. If you have the law, argue law. If you have neither, just argue.'

is at a historic low point in France today. These declarations are crafted by the employees' equivalent of jailhouse lawyers. The result is linguistic gridlock.

Breaking the routine

Yet the exchange of these sterile memos is an essential part of the ritual. Workplace confrontations, which the Anglo-Saxon world has largely set aside in recent years, seem to provide an amusing break from the routine of work. The missing interface between management and employees becomes a genuine problem, however, each time dialogue is called for.

In other cultures, when an employee gets into trouble with management – a warning for poor performance, for example – open communication is normally the quickest route to a solution. But in France the employee under pressure will become a martyr among his mates. A spirit of solidarity springs up in the workplace to protect him, even if he is known to be a drag on the organization; even if *his* non-performance adds to *their* work.

The first time I faced such a case, I realized I had no chance to be viewed as a fair-minded manager. I was expected to be the opposition force in a traditional tug-of-war that I was not aware existed. Everyone else seemed to enjoy it. I was slow to find pleasure in the process.

The legal procedure that follows a warning in a French company is nothing less than surreal for a foreigner accustomed to more efficient corporate justice. After a series of written cautions, the next step in sanctioning the non-performer is a kangaroo court chaired by management, usually the director of human resources. The manager/prosecutor must read out his charges to the 'court' in the presence of the employee, who is backed up with a silent witness – a friend who takes notes in case the proceedings are one day misrepresented by management. After the prosecutor/manager lists the charges (low productivity, slack work habits, bad attitude), the employee takes the floor and denies the charges. Then the head of human resources, in a finger-wagging summary, repeats what the manager said, ignoring the employee's denials. It is an elaborate charade biased in favour of the 'judge', who is part of management and by definition sympathetic to management's position.

The employee's minutes of events, complete with biased versions of the proceedings, is posted the following day on the bulletin board of the '*délégués du personnel*' (the legally constituted employees' organization). Management is of course portrayed as the aggressor, the employee is portrayed as the victim, and the eternal split between the two rolls happily on. Management makes no comment on these minutes.

After two such court sessions, spaced a month or two apart, the employee is normally put on termination notice. Often, however, management will go soft and pay off the non-performer with full indemnities, often topped up with a month or two additional salary in hush money. After meticulously proving a case against an incompetent employee, a private deal is struck whereby the sacking is falsely declared to be a departure by *accord tacit*, a legal formulation that entitles the employee to draw unemployment benefits at 80% of his salary for two years.

False consultation

The serious trouble starts when top management makes a move to reorganize the staff, rationalize the headcount through layoffs, or redirect the objectives of a profit centre. Consultation with employees is part of the process. Employment law in France as in many other countries requires this procedure before plans are finalized, but in fact most of the talk is usually empty and pointless.

In French practice, the workers are allowed to raise objections and propose ways to avoid the sackings. Management is obliged to take these into account but not to the point of implementation. In theory, it is a sensible and honourable process. Of course in reality the plans are finalized beforehand in the executive suite, and the discussion takes place only to satisfy the letter of the law. The dialogue of the deaf can go on for days.

If management attempts to short-circuit the procedure, employees regroup and mobilize, although they are under no illusion as to their power to reverse the process. The hollow discussion throughout the procedure seems to exercise a therapeutic effect on the workers, who play along earnestly.

I had never seen the staff so excited and animated as when just such a circumvention was attempted during my time in France. One woman was to be sacked, and a small, over-staffed department was to be folded into a larger one. Years of pent-up resentment against top management came home to roost. The incident quickly erupted into a strike by the four people concerned, bulletins from the strikers flew around the building for days. The strikers themselves did their best to spread the work stoppage by wandering freely among other departments seeking sympathy. Their action never quite caught on, although eventually a one-hour symbolic work stoppage was organized.

The new challenge to authority created a festive air in the workplace. It was as if the revolution genes in their DNA had been triggered.

Again the missing link caused unnecessary problems. Top management's attitude was to take names and prepare to dismiss them all as soon as things quietened down. But to lower the temperature, one senior manager was delegated to try using his charm to defuse the conflict. Unfortunately he had little charm and less credibility. Employees who had harboured increasing anti-management feelings for years sat in glum silence, impermeable to the speaker's newfound soft-spoken manner. The temperature rose steadily, and the questions and charges became sharper. After two hours, the meeting broke up in disarray.

In the course of the incident, several employees, notably the women, emerged as firebrand defenders of the person to be laid off, rallying the crowd to action with much passion and waving of fists. It was like a scene from the 1920s – smoke-filled rooms, shouting, debating, wild epithets against management, ringing declarations about employees' rights. A labour lawyer was slipped inside the building by the strikers to address a rally. One of the women leaders was nicknamed '*La Pasionaria*', after Dolores Ibarruri, founder of the Spanish Communist Party.

The strikers' position was frankly naive: no company, they argued, should have the right to make economic layoffs unless the company is actually losing money. If there is money in the bank, it should go to employees. In other words, rationalization as a means of preventing financial disaster for the company, or improving its financial performance, was unacceptable. However wrong-headed the position, the oratory was straight out of 1789. It was stirring but rather absurd for the occasion. Management's rigid attitude and long history of arrogance made dialogue impossible. In the end, the mini-reorganization was implemented, and the woman was laid off, but only after she was granted token additional benefits. The employees were jubilant. They had won a small point, and they had enjoyed themselves hugely. They all went back to work as before, but the four strikers, being realists, set about looking for new jobs, and were gone within two months.

Part Two
What Makes Them Tick

5 Managing Uncontrolled Spontaneity

'The French became rebellious because they had
no other way to assert themselves, and they have
remained so.'
André Maurois

Latin cultures are like fire to our ice. The adjustment from one to the other requires heroic flexibility in either direction. The differences are most apparent in attitudes towards the display of emotions.

The basic personality of the southern European is expansive, aggressive, openly affectionate, verbose and volatile. A sudden outburst is often followed by total calm or even warmth, with no apparent memory of the storm that just passed. It is an effective safety valve against emotional overload. The tempestuous side and the calm side can coexist in the southern temperament, creating what seems to a Northerner a compound personality.

The typical northern European worker is more self-contained, repressed, taciturn. He may suffer more in the long run as his anxieties eat up his insides, but the home and the workplace are quieter for it. Whatever his uncertainties or conflicting feelings, he normally will screen thoughts and comments to force the outward impression of consistency and calm. Feelings that don't fit are suppressed. The French, like most Latins, have no such sorting mechanism. What is felt is expelled into the air.

The key, for a northern European or an American working in a Latin culture, is to develop the same short memory – to avoid retaining what has just been said, however disturbing it may have been. Interpersonal relations must be viewed over the long term, smoothing out peaks and valleys of changing moods.

To the Latin, as to the Arab, words are a kind of music. They are used as a show of style and bravado, to make an emotional point. Threats and insults are not to be taken literally. Jacques Chirac, for 20 years one of the country's leading politicians and finally, after three tries, the elected president, made such a violent scene over agricultural policy in Brussels during his tenure as agriculture minister in the 1970s that his German opposite number publicly declared that Chirac needed psychiatric treatment. It was a classic meeting of opposite temperaments – French fire and Germanic ice.

Like Chirac, an employee who allows himself to say outrageous things to a colleague or a manager is probably only letting off steam. In an office situation, sulphurous memos are sometimes exchanged, only to be ignored the next day. A seemingly rocky relationship resumes on an apparently friendly basis. The professional tiff mattered little, as neither party expects friendship to develop anyway.

Volatility as a weapon

Since the French are, in effect, licensed to be volatile, some managers like to use this trait as a weapon to keep subordinates off balance. A division president in one company who enjoys sitting in judgement on his underlings was a fine practitioner of the art. At each executive committee meeting, he would single out the heroes and fools around the table, mixing and matching differently at each meeting with little regard for reality.

To recently appointed members of the committee who thought they had 'arrived', it was unsettling to be kicked around in front of new colleagues. 'One day I am the wisest of the wise. The next day I am a complete nitwit,' one victim complained to me. The technique was intended to prevent the team members from resting on past successes. In fact, the ups and downs of the president became an office joke which everyone nervously tried to laugh off.

In staff meetings, this volatility extends to the entire conference table, regardless of hierarchy. Other foreign managers in France have shared with me this same feeling of rude surprise at the reigning atmosphere. The limits to what is acceptable office behaviour in France are out in the twilight zone for northern Europeans or Americans.

First, a basic rule is that several people talk at the same time with ever-increasing speed and volume. With practice, the foreigner can learn to multiplex his brain, to follow bits of five or six conversations simultaneously. But the ultimate skill is to follow those conversations while also thinking and talking yourself. Few Anglo-Saxon foreigners can do that. Second, table-pounding, gratuitous insults, dirty looks, eye-rolling, brooding, pouting, paper-rustling, hyperventilation – all serve as ways to distance oneself from what is supposed to be going on at the group level.

My first few months were particularly disconcerting. Scanning the faces around the conference table at my weekly staff meeting, I never knew exactly what to expect. To create a soothing atmosphere, I tried the food ploy. I arranged for pots of fresh coffee, and I personally brought in a bag of pastries to the meeting every week. Maybe it was the caffeine, food colouring, or the chemical preservatives, but this little snack only seemed to make the antagonisms worse. Invariably, the tension built up and exploded within the first few minutes. The worst of the shouting matches involved two senior staff members who had a long history of animosity. I never did find out why they hated each other so. Mercifully, one of them eventually resigned.

At this point I made a straightforward appeal to the staff to cut out the backbiting, and to try to work together in peace and harmony towards the obvious common goals.

Spot the invisible barrier

This seemed to calm nerves at first, but after a couple of weeks the hostilities resumed, although at a reduced level.

For an outsider, the problem is to determine how much of this time-consuming foolishness to tolerate. Where is the fine line between playing along with the new culture and being lax in the control of the meeting? It is difficult to be sure.

Touching and feeling

Relations with management are distant, but employees among themselves often express great superficial comradeship. Unlike the British and Americans, they can be affectionate and touchy-feely. Each morning, most of the men kiss most of the women – except the managers, who stand by looking on. It is only a peck on both cheeks, but it is an essential part of the ritual. A chance encounter at midday typically brings an apology, man to woman: 'Oh I haven't given you your kiss today!' Followed by the ritual pecks. In more formal settings, or with special outsiders, hand-kissing is still a gentleman's most elegant gesture of respect for a woman (but for some reason it is considered wrong to do this to a single woman, as I found out when I tried it at an office party).

Being a consensus manager, the double standard rubbed me the wrong way. I knew that office kissing would be too much for my pre-programmed staff to handle, so I broke the mould entirely. I adopted the high-five slap with my younger male staff. They picked up this little bit of Americana, having no preconceptions about it and therefore no defence against it. High-fives are not in the rule book. Imperceptibly, communication crept into a few of our relationships.

Managers, male and female, are far more sedate. They walk around the office or meeting room shaking hands mechanically each morning, a strong squeeze and a couple of pumps, and they exchange a crisp first-name greeting. It is a rather arid ritual in comparison to what goes on down below.

As is true the world over, the French office day starts with agonizing slowness. Colleagues exchange pleasantries and intimacies over strong coffee for the first half hour before settling down to work. Only the subject matter differs. A sampler:

- The fabulous Bourgogne blanc served at last night's dinner.

- A comparison of liver disorders and constipation problems.

- A detailed reivew of who did what over the weekend (Mondays only).

- Among the women, various anecdotes about 'the father of my children' (a term from the new non-married generation).

- Lunch plans. ('You are not going to that awful bistro with the smelly *andouillette*. I can still taste last week's . . .').

And their office neuroses are marginally worse that ours. Many French employees still keep bottles of mineral water on their desks to ward off dehydration or to build up bone marrow, and they worry about the oxygen level in the air and/or the imaginary draughts seeping through the windows. The heavy intake of water is advised by women's magazines, which counsel a litre-and-a-half per day for men and women who work in an air-conditioned office. Most of them manage to consume quantities in that range, making the office loo the busiest place in the building.

The lunch break at midday stops the treadmill and offers a couple of hours of decompression in the lively company of fellow conspirators. The French are known for their critical faculties, and they demonstrate them non-stop, including between gulps of red wine and *steak-frites* at the neighbourhood bistro. And if a business lunch is on the agenda, the venue might be one of the world's finest restaurants. They return to the office energized despite the heavy intake of wine, and managers typically float from meeting to meeting, or burrow away at their paperwork, until 7.30 or 8 pm.

Money can sometimes be an issue, but it is rarely an end in itself. It is the other things that count – childhood friendships, extended families, cinema classics, the country home, weekends in the provinces, and a good connection with the opposite sex. Around my floor in Paris, good books and magazines were everywhere, perhaps because poor quality French television drives people to the printed word. Thick tomes of Stendahl and Victor Hugo lay about the workplace for lunchtime reading by the staff intellectuals. 'Read *Notre Dame de Paris*,' one of my French colleagues told me. 'You will never have to read anything else.'

Naughty marketing

The popular conception of France as a haven of free love is greatly exaggerated. Paris is actually one of the tamer capitals today; Hamburg has long since passed it by in the quality and quantity of sex for sale, or so I am told. But the French have marketed their reputation for naughtiness more cleverly. Anglo-Saxons still think of Paris as the most open city and the French as the world's best lovers.

Corridors in French companies resound with talk of mistresses and boyfriends, but the action, if any, is discreet. There is, however, a willingness to look the other way that British or Americans would have difficulty in mastering. A leading French magazine editor visited New York for a series of interviews with business leaders a few years ago. At grand lunches in New York's skyscrapers he mumbled introductions of his entourage, trailing off as he came to the youngish blonde, whose role was always unclear. Everyone in his group knew that he always travelled with his mistress. The foreigners never seemed to figure it out.

Another leading French editor appointed his wife to edit a new feminist magazine. She became so involved in the subject that she left him to move in with her equally feminist assistant. Paris shrugged it off. Her feminist pretensions made her an exception. What is more striking is that feminism in France is running about 30 years behind the rest of the developed world. French women deny that they are behind; they say they are just different – they have their own style of feminism. Yet women in France still gladly accept remarks that would be actionable in New York or London. To call a woman 'sexy' is still a compliment. An advertising campaign shows a pair of long legs in decorated stockings. The text would cause riots in New York: CHANTAL THOMAS' TIGHTS. THE TIGHTS THAT MAKE ALL THE MEN HAPPY, AND ONE VERY HAPPY.

Television performers use this freedom blatantly. Popular entertainer Jacques Martin welcomed a housewife contestant on stage recently with this admiring exclamation: 'Look at those beautiful legs! Let's give Madame Dupont's legs a big round of applause'. They looked like pretty average legs to me, but the audience enthusiastically obliged.

In the office, it is always open season, at least verbally. Legs, lips, bottoms, necks and knees are fair game for the men's respectful appreciation. To be fair, aside from lyrical exclamations and the usual round of cheek-pecking the fooling around rarely becomes physical. In a business situation, French women who manage men weave a complex web of opposites: dominance and vulnerability, business and personal innuendo, look-but-don't-touch. Women will use all the wiles at their command: the plunging neckline, the hiked-up hemline, lots of jewellery and makeup, the fluttering eyelashes, suggestive comments. In one company, a high-ranking woman and a top male manager had a falling out after an out-of-town management seminar. Within a week, their public demeanour went from pals and partners forever to cats and dogs forever. The company buzzed over the big question: Did he make a move on her, or did he *fail* to make a move on her? No other explanation was even in the running.

Sex, although not rampant, is looked upon as natural and expected. A woman manager was known by the staff to be taking Thursday afternoons off to spend in a hotel with her lover. The prevailing attitude was: 'So what? It seems to do her good'. The missing half-day of work was never contested.

Protecting turf

French white-collar workers cling desperately to their square footage of office space, however cramped. A former Renault high-rise building that my company leased had to be gutted and rebuilt to make way for our new open-plan office design. The Renault space had been honeycombed into hundreds of tiny floor-to-ceiling cubicles with doors and locks. The Renault people spent their day happily closeted, sealed off and in control of their space. Our idea was to go the modern, open-plan way, known in French as '*open-space*', renew the furniture, and create a more harmonious work atmosphere with free communication. When I announced the plan, a groan arose in unison from the staff. They were not convinced. When moving day came six weeks later, they were even less convinced. The parade of protesters through my door in the first days was a chastening experience. A long list of demands included more light fixtures, different light fixtures, more air, more windows, open windows, more partitions, higher partitions, and especially less space for the managers.

When the old desks and chairs were replaced to make the former sweatshop atmosphere of the company more presentable, the intrusion sparked violent resentment. The human resources manager was accosted in the corridors by an employee and accused of high-handed actions detrimental to the well-being of the employees. The subordinate let rip: 'How dare you decide what colour my desk should be!' The human resources man, incredulous, replied: 'And we thought you would be pleased'. Another woman, unhappy with the placement of her desk, announced to me that she would be resigning in protest just as fast as she could find another job, and she had a good prospect. The intensity of her tantrum left me shaking.

There was no choice but to order a dozen new partitions to break up the space, thereby diluting the effect of the design by about half. Now we were all half-happy.

6 Privacy: Don't Ask Me Where I Live

'As a general rule, office life and private life should
be kept entirely separate.'

Gisèle d'Assailly in *Le Savoir-Vivre*

A friend in Paris told me this story: The president of an American company's French office was a newly arrived Yank from Detroit. His father had been born in England, which made him 'European' in the eyes of his company. His ersatz Englishness, in fact, seemed to be his main qualification for this new cross-cultural task. He spoke French without shame, in the jokey way Maurice Chevalier used to speak English. He was open and friendly with all comers. His company considered him to be just the man for Paris.

Three weeks into the assignment, the American created panic among his staff when he invited everyone at head office to his home with spouses for an old-fashioned American house-warming party one Sunday afternoon. He had forgotten that Paris is not the American Midwest. He and his wife were all teeth and hair. Their broad, American smiles never slackened throughout the party, so overcome were they by the hundred per cent attendance. They said they felt something like love radiating from their new happy family of employees.

The event was, of course, anguish for the French. People who had never crossed paths outside the office spent the afternoon moving crabwise around the edges of the room to avoid contact with various untouchables below and above them in the office structure. The presence of their spouses was a keen source of discomfort for most of the employees. They seemed to feel that by displaying their partners in public they were lowering their personal defences, making themselves more vulnerable.

The next day, the American was taken aside by his French second-in-command and advised not to try it again. The American was bewildered. All he had seen were *their* smiles reflecting *his* smiles. The Frenchman tried his best to explain the Chinese Wall that separates private and professional life. The American found it hard to believe, but he accepted the obvious reality and retreated internally.

The story illustrates one of the first traps a foreign manager in France will fall into: violation of personal privacy. You are not expected to share your personal details, nor ask them of your new acquaintances. Your French contacts probably do not want intimacy. They are using their code of conversational behaviour to maintain distance from you, and it is important not to be offended. Remember, they do it to their friends, too. It can be a difficult adjustment for the uninitiated. Casual chit-chat with strangers at a dinner party becomes an arduous exercise in non-communication. Only safe subjects such as the weather, the cinema, the theatre or books are recommended until the bonds of friendship can take hold. In France, this may be a matter of years.

Getting too personal

Of all the things considered impolite in France, one of the worst gaffes can be to ask a Frenchman what his job is. I once tried it, to be told by a wealthy, perfumed gentleman, '*Je ne suis qu'un bricoleur*'. ('I'm only a handyman.') My failing ears heard '*cambrioleur*' (burglar), which I knew couldn't be right. So I switched quickly to an analysis of the week's weather. Later I learned that the man owned three blocks of expensive apartment houses in the exclusive suburb of Neuilly. To keep himself occupied, he did many of the small repairs on plumbing and electrical installations himself. I suppose he thought of himself as a kind of handyman, at least compared to his brother-in-law, who was a lawyer and a prominent Senator. But without intending to, he had left me feeling confused over how to reach him, even on a superficial level. What I had not appreciated was that he had no desire to be reached. Quite the contrary. He was keeping himself well out of reach.

The barriers the French erect around themselves take a special form at work. The aim is to make a clear demarcation between business life and personal life, thereby limiting the unseen enemy's angles of attack. Even with members of my own staff, I apparently had no right to ask direct questions. A few weeks after my arrival, I found myself on a train sitting beside one of my more talented female writers. To pass the time, after I had exhausted all the polite public subjects I could think of, I asked her to tell me a bit about herself.

'I certainly will not,' she said, stiffening. 'You need to know only one thing about me – how well I work. The rest is my business.'

I guess she had a point. Perhaps she had been brought up on a French manual on good manners that makes this extraordinary assertion: 'True good manners dictate that one never asks questions'. The same book advises men and women never to give their names to strangers, including strangers at work. 'It is a simple matter of caution. You never know whom you might be speaking to.'

Separating work life from professional life can be desirable to a degree, of course. People who keep their private lives in different compartments may well end up more rounded and ultimately more satisfied with their lives. Business is not everything to them.[1] Even some Americans believe better balance is called for in the US system. American Jeffrey Salkin, who has written on the relationship of work and personal growth in the United States, sounded this alarm in a recent article: 'I meet many people who are disillusioned with their professions. They sense that they are spiritually damaged by the pernicious cycle of working, wanting and having as ends in themselves.'

See you tomorrow

In Paris, there is no such danger. But there are other effects that flow from the suppression of normal human relations at work. The barriers are most formidable among workers and especially between workers and managers. Even the most balanced US-trained managers tend to think of this as needlessly divisive. The American view is that if barriers are erected too high, they prevent colleagues in the workplace from ever getting to know each other. Human understanding between the levels of manager and employee is thus prevented from flowering, and this in turn leads to a greater risk of misunderstanding on work matters. One American woman in Paris summed it up after a few years of observing this iron curtain between work life and private life: 'At the end of the work day, my French colleagues put on their hats and coats, turn to me and say in the friendliest way, "*Au revoir. A demain.*" And they mean it.'

The taboos against sharing the details of one's private life are much less present in the Anglo-Saxon countries. Friendships, love affairs and marriages commonly grow out of office relationships. Some multinationals

---

1 The passion for privacy has its variations in France. In the provinces, where outside distractions are scarce, private and professional lives naturally overlap to a greater degree.

such as IBM and General Motors and the entrepreneurial companies of the high technology industries actively encourage employees to intermingle on evenings and weekends. The old ITT used to call together its European headquarters people once a year at a July 4th picnic near Brussels where everyone pretended to be American for a day. Beer, hot dogs and picnic games were regular features of the celebration. In many such companies, directories of employees' home addresses, phone numbers and spouses' names – from secretaries to the chairman – are often freely distributed. And they are not just for Christmas card lists.

Rosabeth Moss Kanter, Harvard Business School professor and former editor of the *Harvard Business Review*, notes that heavy off-the-job socializing is a hallmark of innovative US organizations. These connections, she says, serve 'an important task-related purpose: building a foundation of cross-cutting relationships to make integrative team formation that much easier'.

In France, the reflex is to resist togetherness, whatever the consequences. Professional life has its place, but it must not encroach on private life. Friends come from a separate stream of life reaching back to childhood and family relationships. Professional contacts take their place later in life, and co-exist on a separate level. An American manager who was new to French companies finally grasped this issue when he asked his secretary to collect the home telephone numbers of his key people. She reported back two days later with 2 out of 14. The other 12 grudgingly relented after the manager made the request person-to-person over the next few days, pledging not to use the numbers unnecessarily, and swearing never to pass them on to third parties. Without meaning to, he left the employees feeling invaded.

Drawing the line

I had trouble getting to grips with this separation of what I had always thought of as a continuum – private and business life. Early in my stay in France, I made a modest proposal that the closing dinner of a company-sponsored seminar include spouses.

'I'll think it over, but I am doubtful,' my boss told me. 'This is not usually done in France.' My egalitarian idea was never rejected, it simply was never mentioned again.

The most harmless brush with an employee's private life is quickly squelched. Making small talk, I once proposed to one of my most senior deputies that the two of us organize an evening with our wives. His reaction was non-committal. When I asked him a few days later to remind me of the name of his wife, his icy reply was unmistakable: 'Her name is the same as mine'. I think I got the message. My attentions were at least unwanted, and possibly misinterpreted.

I learned another lesson from one of my more promising young writers who had just returned from a sick leave of several weeks. He dropped by the office for lunch with his closest colleagues a day or two before resuming work. In my office afterwards, I told him how pleased I had been to see the warmth and friendship the staff was displaying to him. The young man shot back, a bit too fast, I thought: 'These people are not my friends,' he said. 'They are only my co-workers. My friends are the people I see in my private life, which has nothing at all to do with my work here.' To me, it sounded like a double life, but in fact it was only my cognitive dissonance jangling in the background again.

After 15 months with the company, I still had never seen the inside of any of my superiors' or employees' homes. In a poignant touch during my last week, one of my staff did drive me in his car to a farewell lunch, pointing out however that I was the only person from the company he had ever allowed in it. I blushed, he flattered me so. But I still did not know, in several cases, who was married, who had children, who was not married and had children, who was gay and who was straight. The most bizarre case of personal secrecy was a woman employee who hitched a ride home with me after we had worked together until midnight one night. She alighted at the entrance of Montmartre Cemetery rather than indicate her exact street. I lost sight of her as she went whistling past the gravestones into the inky darkness. It was with some relief that I saw her reappear in the office the following morning unhurt and all smiles.

A 'calculative' relationship

The compartmentalization of the two lives translates into a lesser degree of solidarity with the objectives of the company than is commonly found in the US or Britain. French employees show little concern for the greater good of the firm. The employee wants to know what the company can do for him. The other question – what he can do for the company – is not his concern. As Jay Szarka of the University of Bath writes: The employee's relationship with the company 'does not involve a moral commitment, but is primarily calculative'. That is, the highly individualistic French worker goes along with the company only as long as his goals and the company's goals coincide. Normally this is not very far.

Although this is not to say the French do not work hard, in fact one result of their attitude is that they have not developed the dependency on work (workaholism) that Americans have. Manufacturing employees in the United States now work 320 hours a year more than the French, the equivalent of two additional months.

Consistent with this arm's-length relationship, the French employee

HERE'S THE DEAL. YOU TELL ME
EXACTLY WHAT YOU WANT ME
TO DO, AND I'LL DO IT IF I
FEEL LIKE IT.

Déresponsabilisation

will often do his best to dodge responsibility. He knows instinctively that he must prevent the company from taking over his life. The job description, therefore, becomes a strict framework for his professional life. He chooses to revel in these limitations, and refuses to give himself to the company. The flowering of his individuality, a highly prized French character trait, will be reserved for his private life and his private friends. The ideal job is considered to be one in which airtight parameters are spelled out, hour-to-hour duties are listed, and performance criteria are detailed down to the last erg. Once this is achieved, the employee has been blissfully *déresponsabilisé*. He is comforted by the limits of the job, and will refuse to cross the boundaries into the realm of initiative.

This attitude echoes the findings of Geert Hofstede, the Dutch specialist in cultural comparisons, who studied 'uncertainty avoidance' (or, put another way, the need for predictability) among employees of IBM worldwide and ranked the results by country. He defines the phenomenon as the extent to which members of a culture feel threatened by uncertain or unknown situations. The feeling, he says, is expressed by nervous stress and a need for written and unwritten rules. The opposite of this attitude might be a sense of adventure in one's professional life – being comfortable with the idea of surprises, even bad surprises, in career development.

An interesting contrast to France is the attitude of top managers at McGraw-Hill Inc., a US publishing company where I once worked. These men were in and out of power with the briskness of a revolving door. Senior staff, far from fretting over the uncertainties, often joked about the parlous situation in which they found themselves the moment they failed to make their quarterly numbers. A typical philosophy was the jaunty attitude of one of the corporate vice presidents: 'I knew this job was dangerous when I took it'. A French manager would find this degree of uncertainty unbearable.

In search of certainty

Indeed, the French came out in Hofstede's study as among the world's most surprise-averse. In his now well-established Uncertainty Avoidance Index, France ranked near the top in the craving for predictability – tenth out of fifty-three countries studied. Germany came in twenty-ninth, the United States forty-third, and Britain forty-seventh. The least concerned about predictability was Singapore, a virtual police state which also has a growing economy and suffers from a labour shortage. Very little is uncertain in Singapore, so the population is unconcerned about it.

In France, the urge to be free of responsibility poses just one more obstacle to managers' efforts to make the productivity machine function optimally. Any new duties imposed by management are likely to trigger a demand for additional compensation, and without delay. Vague promises of a salary review will not suffice. Employees on several occasions put the question to me directly: 'Why should I do more for the company at the same pay?' In the very different world of Anglo-Saxony, the assumption that a bigger job well done will lead to better things seems naive to the French employee.

Even with the parameters of a job nailed down, however, management cannot count on the basic task being accomplished. As heirs to the Revolution, the employees reserve the right to march to their own drummer. Frequently, the line between individuality and outright bloody-mindedness is blurred. One young professional explained to me the French attitude towards work, half in jest, shortly after I arrived:

'*Dites-moi exactement ce que vous voulez que je fasse, et je le ferai si j'ai envie.*' ('Tell me exactly what you want me to do, and I'll do it if I feel like it.')

7 Considering 'Foolish Consistency'

'If Paris was the world capital of Cartesian reason, it was also the capital of astrology, fringe-medicine and pseudo-scientific religiosity. There was, and still is, a strong anti-rationalist culture in France.'

Paul Johnson

One quality the Mediterranean peoples have brought to the world is the ability to live comfortably with inconsistency. The Greeks have it, the Italians have it, and certainly the French do. To northern Europeans, this ability sometimes looks more like confusion, self-doubt, or possibly mental illness. But it is not. The French wear their inconsistencies well. Their light-and-shade, brutal-and-gentle, rational-irrational combinations have spawned many shelves of learned books. Indeed, their very ability to coast through life in an apparently contradictory state of mind is attractive to many from northern Europe, where the culture affords no such luxury.

Exaggerated politeness concealing an often contemptuous view of others is but one example. Embedded beneath the French outer stiffness is a full set of Old World manners and values. Hand-kissing is widely practised, and men will fall over themselves to hold doors open for women. The dreaded mother-in-law is called *belle-mère* (beautiful mother). Forms of address to strangers (*'Je vous en prie, Monsieur.'* *'Auriez-vous la gentillesse de me donner son numéro de téléphone?'* *'Excusez-moi de vous déranger, Monsieur.'* *'Merci mille fois.'*) are music to the ears of Americans and Britons who have been de-mannered by the brusqueness, the stress and the false familiarity of business life at home. But it can be confusing when these same people who are clothed in such worldly, exquisite manners turn out to be explosively obscene and aggressive towards drivers who cut them off in traffic.

Doubletalk in business

In a business setting, these two behaviours can be applied with chilling grace. A French manager can sometimes deal harshly with a troublesome underling, oozing charm while twisting the knife. A boss telling a subordinate for the third time how to do a job might preface his instructions with, *'Je me suis sans doute mal exprimé'*. ('No doubt I expressed myself badly.') The employee hears these words in their true meaning: 'This is the last time I will warn you, stupid person, then you're on your own'. And a hare-brained proposal will be deflected ever so elegantly before being trashed: *'Votre idée, mon ami, n'est pas inintéressante.'* ('Your idea, my friend, is not uninteresting.') The astute listener hears another meaning: 'My three-year-old could do better than that, smart guy'.

Polite formulations on paper are ritualized far beyond the US or British practice. Linguistic customs in business correspondence seem especially refined. How else to characterize the typical last paragraph of a routine letter: 'I beg you, sir, to accept the expression of my highest esteem'? The previous paragraph might have been threatening or critical, but the ending must never vary. Even if centuries of repetition have taken the sincerity out of the respectful words, the rite has its own importance. The proof: omitting that last sentence from a letter is an inexcusable lapse.

Forms of politesse are so extreme that office wits in France sometimes mock themselves on the subject. Faking obsequiousness, they will approach co-workers with this opening line: *'Monsieur, excusez-moi de vous demander pardon, mais . . .'* ('Sir, forgive me for begging your pardon, but . . .').

Other level-headed features of these emotional people tend to impress the foreigner favourably. The logical, Cartesian thought processes taught in the French school system help to structure problem-solving and business meetings, although no records for speed will be set. French business memo-writing is such a demanding exercise in logic that I had to struggle to master it. My casual tone and untidy habits of expression made me feel like a schoolboy until I straightened up. One superior, reviewing my memo, politely told me, 'You had best rewrite this or you will be machine-gunned at the board meeting, my friend'.

Unreason ascending

It is especially refreshing to live in a society that rejects the rational as the only legitimate framework for modern life. The weekly newsmagazine *Le Point* published a cover story inviting readers to 'Plunge into the Irrational'. The appeal of the unexplainable is more present than ever in France today.

Seemingly in contradiction to the worship of logic, the French give a much more privileged place than the British or Americans to mystery, chance and, more recently, to spiritualism. Dreams of good fortune are part of the search for inner peace that will help overcome the cruel realities of daily life, and these dreams can come from many sources.

Gambling, small and large, is omnipresent, with organized betting available on anything that moves. The French National Lottery is one of the world's oldest, tracing its origins back to Louis XIV; *pari-mutuel* betting on horses is a national pastime; the 138 casinos (the highest number in Europe) do a booming business throughout the country. Banco, Tac O Tac, Loto and various televised games of chance have proliferated and attracted record numbers of steady customers in the past ten years. About 20 million French people now bet regularly in some form. The total invested in gambling is estimated at 70 billion francs (about 9 billion pounds) a year.

Acceptance of the irrational sometimes leads to unhappy results. An ageing blonde TV celebrity landed in criminal court for her role in the marketing of a cheap, gold-plated ring that was supposed to cure the purchaser's physical and mental ills. Thousands of suckers saw the advertising in national magazines, bought the ring, and were surprised to find that it didn't work. One of them decided to prosecute. The girl escaped a jail term only because she was a celebrity and was thought to be none too bright herself.

Anglo-Saxons in Paris often come round to the belief that perhaps the French are on to something good in their fascination with the irrational. Throwing off the chains of reason makes for a more easygoing approach to life's insoluble problems, and especially to the erratic behaviour of others. One well-adjusted expatriate in Paris who works for a relocation agency says she has lowered her blood pressure significantly by refusing to seek explanations for the way things work and the way people behave. She answers foreigners' 'Why?' questions about peculiar French institutions and behaviour with the simple answer, 'Because'.

Reason as a recent phenomenon

In a strange way, for a dry, numbers-orientated Anglo-Saxon, this spooky world is part harmless fun, part spiritual succour. If nothing else, it relieves the brain of the tyranny of thinking through all of the world's problems. We sometimes forget that Western civilization's commitment to science and reason is barely one hundred years old.

Although the French can claim credit for launching the Enlightenment period in the eighteenth century, the general population of the Western world did not really emerge into the Age of Reason until the early-twentieth century, and even then with reservations in large parts of the population. Darwin, Freud and Einstein together managed to explain most of the mysteries of the physical and psychological worlds, but somehow many people still needed spiritual nurturing.

Naked handwriting

Flirting with obscurantism seems to do it for the French, extending even to the dubious art of handwriting analysis. Nearly all French companies now require handwriting samples as part of the recruitment process. Human resources officers demand a handwritten letter for examination by a 'grapho' who will puzzle over the half-crossed 't's and the bountiful loops to produce a detailed report revealing many indiscreet things about you. The graphologist will leave huge gaps on key behavioural questions but oddly enough manages to include some accurate insights. (The analysis of my scrawl correctly said I was a consensus manager but failed to note, thank God, that I was weak in maths, that I hated writing and that I was facing an impossible cultural challenge.) In most other countries, graphology is rightly shunned as unscientific and unreliable, or at the very least an invasion of privacy. But the French want desperately to believe in it. In some ways their enthusiasm seems forced. As if privately aware of its unreliability, many companies will commission two experts – one known for his toughness, one known for his sweetness. The contrasting reports are then weighed and averaged to get at whatever 'truth' is desired.

The fact that two graphologists disagree wildly on the meaning of the loops and whorls in personal handwriting does not cause undue concern. The mere fact that the applicant's personality has been plumbed by handwriting experts provides the company with a scientific sense, however shaky, about the future employee's psychic makeup. The report is popped into the person's confidential file for the exclusive use of the company.

Employees who request copies of their analysis are usually refused access or made to jump through legal hoops to get at it. The company thus manages the individual with secret, spurious knowledge of a personality profile that remains hidden from the employee.

A spreading tendency

It is more disturbing to watch the element of mysticism spread into new domains little by little. Just in the past few years, business has conferred upon the occult a new legitimacy. Some companies now ask applicants for their astrological sign, and ponder the alignment of planets with that of their future co-workers to measure their eventual compatibility. An estimated 10 million French people (about one in five) consult astrologers or clairvoyants regularly. Alternative medicine is sweeping the country, with growing clientele for acupuncture, phytotherapy, instinctotherapy, thalasotherapy. What will be next? Pulverised tiger bones? Tea leaves?

Who could have predicted that a seemingly homogenous, stable Catholic

An attraction for the occult

country (80% call themselves church members) could accommodate 25,000 sects, ranging from oriental religions to scientology and Jehovah's Witnesses? About 50,000 people make a living in France off some form of occult activity, twice the number of practising Catholic priests. Some other curious numbers:

- 81% of the French believe that science will never explain everything.

- 42% believe in the curative powers of magnetism and the laying on of hands.

- 37% believe in the predictions of astrologists.

- 32% believe it is bad luck to put a loaf of bread on the table upside down.

- 29% believe the devil definitely or probably exists.

- 25% believe in fortune-tellers.

- 23% believe it is good luck to step in dog droppings with the left foot.

- 20% believe in palmistry and numerology.

For a Frenchman, these many paradoxes can coexist comfortably because consistency for its own sake, or 'foolish consistency' as Emerson called it, is not considered a virtue in France. The contradictions of the human condition are on public display. (Anglo-Saxons may have the same contradictions, but will suppress them.) So a veneer of politeness resides happily alongside a volatile national temperament; a reverence for logic does not exclude the appeal of mystery; xenophobia and red-neck racism are covered by a layer of sophistication and worldliness; a lacklustre professional life conceals an active and vigorous private life. France is probably no more complex than other countries, it only seems so because the inconsistencies are displayed for all to see.

8 Elitism at its Best and Worst

'Rarely do bosses in tradition-bound organizations actually
have to say "no" directly to a subordinate's idea. A few well-placed
frowns or eyebrow raises, some pregnant pauses, a reiteration of
the real assignment, and citation of accumulated years of company
wisdom can be enough to make it clear to people that new ideas
are not welcome.'

Rosabeth Moss Kanter

It is one of the highlights of the Champs Elysées parade on Bastille Day, the 14th of July. In military formation, the sword-bearing young men and a few women in navy blue uniforms and three-cornered caps march in step down the boulevard, taking applause from the patriots and tourists. These strangely decked-out folk are not soldiers or sailors. They are the future captains of industry and government, students of l'Ecole Polytechnique. They symbolize perhaps the single most contradictory institution in the country, the managerial *élite* that is trying to take France into the twenty-first century by looking back to the nineteenth.

X, as the school is known for its emblem of crossed swords, is part of a slightly wider super-*élite* postgraduate system that includes three other *grandes écoles*, the Ecole Nationale d'Administration (ENA), the Ecole Normale Supérieure (Normale Sup) and the Ecole des Hautes Etudes Commerciales (HEC). A benchmark study a few years ago by Leslie Mitchell de Quillacq identified those who matter in French finance and how they got there. The common denominator among her 27 most influential men was that most (22 of them) had gone through the rigorous formation of at least one of the three leading *grandes écoles*. Only two on the list skipped all the big schools. One of them was Jimmy Goldsmith, but he managed to muddle through with other advantages.

When X was established by Napoleon, its aim was to give France an educated ruling class that was non-aristocratic, non-clerical and nationalist. The system has succeeded on all three scores but in the process created a different aristocracy with many of the evils of the old class. The French *élite* now operate within a caste system: they talk mostly to each other, they solve problems the same way, and they have a largely uniform vision of France. While not every French manager has attended the top schools, the less privileged members of the managerial class have taken on many of the élitist trappings.

The system contrasts starkly with the more meritocratic paths to power in the United States and even in class-ridden Great Britain. Political and business leaders of both nations come from a mixture of backgrounds, often underprivileged, ensuring two important positive features: that talented people from all walks of life have an opportunity to excel, and that the resulting pool of ideas tends to be more varied. To be fair, a sign of change in France is the growing wave of criticism and resentment against the suffocating effects of X and other top schools. Many thoughtful French people are pressing for reform to end what Jean-Michel Gaillard calls in his book, *Tu seras président, mon fils* (You will be President, My Son), 'clearly an abuse of their dominant position'.

A second correcting force is the prosecution of some of these previously untouchable executives for questionable ethical practices. A clean-up movement by the French judiciary against the private use of company funds and the bending of accounting rules has sent a chill through the managerial ranks. Over time, traditional privileges will surely erode as France makes the transition to a more liberal model.

The ultimate networks

But the fact remains that today's *élite* is still composed of men holding these diplomas and belonging to these networks. Through their alumni associations and other exclusive clubs, they are virtually guaranteed lifetime employment in top positions, thereby blocking the way of other talented men and women who might be more innovative. Successful top-management careers in the leading companies still depend to a great extent on university and graduate school connections, as they have for more than one hundred years.

'France's top executives are reputedly among the best-educated in the world,' wrote Jean-Louis Barsoux and Peter Lawrence in a study of French management published in 1990. Despite the weaknesses of the system, there is no denying that it produces admirable graduates. Foreign executives who might have made their mark merely though business performance will find it difficult to keep pace with the quick minds and rich intellectual backgrounds of these erudite men and women.

Just keeping up with high-level cultural allusions in a French business meeting can be taxing. When I first began dealing with the French in the 1970s, I found myself nodding and agreeing more often than initiating cultured repartee. As the saying goes, it is better to remain silent and be suspected of being dim than to speak up and remove all doubt. The cultural and literary references flying about have the effect, wanted or not, of screening the unworthy from the executive suite. A foreigner, who may have accumulated an equally impressive set of references from his own culture, will meet with an unforgiving gaze if he tries to chip in with some unfamiliar nuggets. To compete, it would be wise to brush up on your Voltaire, your Napoleonic wars, and your knowledge of the French Revolution.

To the French, it is not pretentious to pause amid a discussion of business strategy and quote the poet Virgil in the original Latin. A French executive might call a major challenge a '*situation Corneillienne*' after the plots of the classic French playwright. *Bons mots* from Racine and Rabelais will be flicked into the conversation.

The prestigious university degree has long been a guarantee of a fast-track career in top management in the country's most important firms. Armed with the diploma, the young graduate sits back and waits for employers to seek him out for positions that guarantee top salaries and heavy responsibility. This is not mere networking, this is a self-perpetuating club of management snobs with lifetime membership. If one of the *grandes écoles* graduates loses his job in Company A, he is sure to be quickly rescued by a classmate in Company B. Whether good education ensures good management is a burning question in France today, but the erudition is a wonder to observe for foreigners coming from less academic backgrounds.

Of course like most developed countries, the era of the self-taught entrepreneur has dawned, if somewhat timidly, in France, too. A few self-made men and women have made successful careers in the past few years. Francis Baygues, Bernard Tapie and Francine Gomez are the three nearly always cited to prove the point. But Mme Gomez sold her Waterman pen company to Gillette (then failed in her attempt to start a hotel business for the *élite*), Tapie has been tainted with scandal and declared bankrupt, and the late M. Baygues' heirs face charges of corporate misconduct. There may be a few more somewhere in the provinces, but the élitist system remains very much intact and dominant.

Shameful impulses, like the libido

In France, business problems tend to be solved by looking at how past problems were solved – the old rear-view-mirror style of driving that business gurus warn against. As a result, young people who bring new solutions face a formidable barrier. The similar backgrounds and training of the managerial *élite* create a convenient but dangerous closed-circuit life that is rarely challenged by new thinking. Big companies in other countries sometimes fall victim to this OBS (One Big Solution) syndrome. But in France, it is institutionalized and programmed by the standardized training. There is no room for discussion. Translated into management techniques, it leads to a win/lose, top-down approach – techniques that are increasingly discredited outside of France.

A curious case in point arose in 1989 when the state-owned electronics and appliances giant, Groupe Thomson, was forced by the government to take a 21.6% share in Crédit Lyonnais to shore up the bank's capital after a hard year. Thomson was given no say in management of the bank and only got a seat on the board six years later. The bank's performance has continued to spiral downward, taking Thomson into red ink with it.

Again in 1991, Thomson found itself fending off unwanted government attention when its own financial problems were nearly resolved by a *dirigiste* decree: the money-losing part of Thomson was ordered by the Prime Minister's office to be detached and grafted on to another state company that had spare cash. Some 60,000 employees learned from one day to the next that they were to be working for a new proprietor. The problem-solvers from the big schools nearly prevailed, but valuation and accounting problems later forced a rethinking of the plan. Such cavalier shuffling of large business units seems unthinkable in other modern economies.

At this writing, Thomson was again the object of government attention. Chairman Alain Gomez was sacked in an eight-minute audience with Prime Minister Alain Juppé, and Thomson was declared heading for privatization. As part of the same *dirigiste* decree, the two giant defence contractors Dassault and Aérospatiale were instructed to merge. It is hard to imagine another developed country subject to such direct control from the prime minister's office. Market forces, the proven driver of efficiency in business for more than 200 years, still take a back seat to the thinking of the *élite* in France.

The entrenchment of the top echelon is another barrier to mobility in French society. Alain Peyrefitte, a former government minister and now a member of the Académie Française, has written about the *élite* in categorical terms: 'Our anti-economic attitudes have been formed and are still maintained by the influence of the various *élites*.' In French history, much as in Britain, it was socially incorrect to dirty one's hands in commerce, he notes. These taboos still linger visibly.

Even today, Peyrefitte finds the influence detrimental, to say the least: 'In general terms, economic motives are in the same class as the libido. Our hierarchical societies have suppressed them for centuries in a system

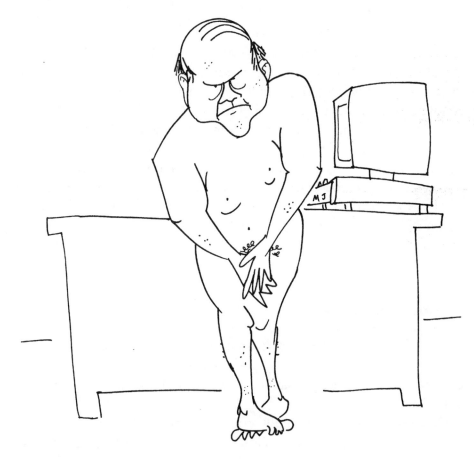

"ECONOMIC MOTIVES ARE IN THE SAME CLASS AS THE LIBIDO."

The shame of being in business

of complexes. We will not become an adult society, and we will not overcome our lag, unless we free ourselves from these taboos.'

How the club works

The men of the *élite*, and they are nearly all men, live in a vacuum-sealed world, soaring above the fray of day-to-day business. They separate themselves from lesser beings in meetings and on social occasions. A top manager of a major company will be eager to drop names of the other top managers around Paris who were in his *promotion*, his graduating class at the Polytechnique or ENA of 30 or 40 years ago. The listener gradually realizes he is being excluded from an invisible club.

Strange, coded communication transpires at this altitude among the *grands seigneurs*. In one curious incident to which I was witness, two of these barons found underlings in their companies in conflict. Rather than endure a confrontation with a school friend, Baron No. 1 sent by courier a blunt letter to Baron No. 2, inscribed in the margin by his own hand, in pencil: '*Cher ami*, I intercepted this letter from my chief executive, and decided not to send it to you. Perhaps you could look into the problem and let me know what you think.' The result was that three drones at division level in the receiving company spent half a day drafting a reply, which Baron No. 2 then sent winging back to Baron No. 1 inscribed with a similar hands-off covering note. When the barons resolved the problem, their wishes became the command of each level below.

An abortive attempt

To be sure, top management in some companies in France is moving towards a lowering of the traditional barriers that separate them from employees. Too much isolation is recognized by the progressive as unhealthy.

One woman at the top who worries about her seclusion decided to do something about it. On two occasions over a period of two months she descended from her suite of top-floor offices to sweep through the maze of desks and partitions on the main floor of her division. It was a brave attempt at MBWA, management by walking around, American-style. Try as she would, however, neither she nor the employees could handle it. She returned from her second tour in a state of agitation.

'I am shocked. My people are afraid of me. Somebody even addressed me as *Madame Présidente*,' she confided to a colleague.

In the end, she could not surmount the cultural barriers. She was right about the impression she had made. She was only wrong to be surprised. Reaction among the staff ranged from suspicion that she was spying on them (more *flicage*) to remarks that she must be softening up the staff because she wants something from them. As one employee remarked, 'At least she could slow down and say hello to us'. She never made a third foray. Distance was the expected behaviour, and everyone was more comfortable with that.

It is important to a French manager to be seen to hold great power. If a manager is perceived as the puppet of the next level up, employees will tend to circumvent him, knowing that he occupies only an intermediate stage of authority. To deal with this stigma – which after all everyone carries, even the chairman, who fears the shareholders – I heard myself in meetings with my staff saying over and over, 'I am nobody's *marionette*'. Although I wasn't, some of them never believed me. Only when I left the company did the doubters come and congratulate me on my moral rectitude. It was strange indeed to be praised for dropping out of the game.

To be known as an *exécutant* and not a *décideur* is management suicide. The French manager has a curious way of dealing with this problem. In the process of executing orders from above – and most of the orders come from high up the pyramid – each manager will transmit the received wisdom in the first person: 'I have decided . . .', 'I am asking you . . . ', 'My plan for the future . . . '. This grammatical construction is essential to preserve one's authority. Managers will use it even for orders that contradict last week's plan and that the manager finds ridiculous. Every decision must be conveyed as the manager's own, not as the latest word from headquarters.

To be exposed as an *exécutant* is the beginning of the end. The apparent zigzags in thought and action only add to the mystique of the manager, thus widening the gulf that separates him from the people he is trying to motivate.

Part Three

Eating and Talking – What They Do Best

9 How Quickly the Barriers Crumble

'You could write a history of Paris on the basis of what
went on in its restaurants and cafés.'
                                                    Waverly Root

'I am tired of French eating, the messes, the sauces, greases
&c. combined with the extreme predilection for the table, of
the natives, male and female, who all look red and fat while
they sit there.'
                                                    Henry James

In the close quarters and low lights of the multi-starred restaurants all over
Paris, the thick layers of French defence mechanisms magically fall away
every day between 1 pm and 3 pm. It is time for the business lunch, the
great leveller. Sharing a meal together forces all present into a social
setting that instantly – if temporarily – truncates the normal stages of a
developing relationship. A foreigner needs to do his homework, but if he
can participate in the cultural commentary and the food-banter he will find
the luncheon *ambience* the best setting in France for facilitating open
communication.

In terms of cuisine, world standards for the business lunch are set in
Paris, although other cultures have their imitations. Indeed, the very term
'business lunch' is too pedestrian for the French version. What happens is
no mere intake of fuel. Henry James's critical view notwithstanding, it is
a sensory, personal and professional experience so sophisticated and so
critical that it can change your life.

More good or bad can be done to a business relationship in the two
hours at the table than in two months of ordinary business dealings across
a seven-foot mahogany desk. Lunch is an opportunity to display one's
culture and refinement in addition to covering a few obligatory business
topics. With defences checked at the door, table talk usually focuses on
casual subjects, culture, private life and especially food in that period of
limbo before the main course arrives (some say this friendly period lasts
until dessert). I can think of no other setting where private subjects can be
broached so fast with new French acquaintances. It was over lunch that I
learned that my dining companion was a closet hot-air balloon pilot. It was

over lunch that a high-flying woman communications director told me wistfully that her *homme* would probably never marry her. And it was over lunch with a leading French industrialist that I learned of his quest for the perfect *salade niçoise,* his private do-it-yourself passion at weekends.

'Eating is a convivial affair', noted Barsoux and Lawrence in their book *Management in France.* 'The French enjoy talking about food in much the same way as the British find diversion in the weather – these are topics which unify a nation.' To which I would only add that they enjoy talking, full stop – and their cultural barriers give them precious few outlets. The business lunch is their safety valve.

Neutral territory for guests

Restaurants in France were until recently the only place for entertaining business contacts. The private home was out of bounds, a sacred, secret place for close family and childhood friends. This is less true today, as France slowly loosens up, but none the less business associates are rarely invited elsewhere than to public restaurants.

Middle managers climbing their way up the company ladder select their restaurants as carefully as a Londoner selects his club. In France, everyone is watching and waiting for him to announce his selection. Senior managers are equally careful, but they use the choice as a way of dispensing favour on the underling or customer. It is a good way to put your young thrusters in their place. When a superior says, 'Let's just grab a *steak-frites* at the corner café', he may be telling you something unpleasant.

In my earlier incarnation as a *Business Week* reporter in France, an interview subject chose an exquisite form of put-down on me, then a lowly journalist. After I had written a story that ruffled his feathers, he invited me to lunch, ordered sandwiches in his office, then insisted that I eat alone while he talked, as he was too busy to eat. I got no pleasure out of the experience. To make matters worse, the French have never mastered the art of the sandwich.

In recent years, lunching at the office has become more fashionable, but as always there is an interesting French twist. In my research for this book, I enjoyed one such catered 'cold' lunch at the offices of Inter-Cultural Management, Avenue de l'Opéra, in central Paris. The cold salmon and fresh mayonnaise were succulent, and the white wine was top quality. It all came handsomely packed in a smart cardboard box. The London equivalent might be two soggy sandwiches dripping with Day-Glo orange chicken tikka bits.

For those who make use of the wide world of Parisian restaurants, special antennae are required. The 'in' places change constantly as the fickle public searches for new sensations and new settings for this important ceremony. At a proper lunch, rarely does the bill come in under 500 francs a head, and the company is happy to pay. The cognoscenti know that they must avoid Maxim's, which is for the Arabs and the Japanese. Fouquet's on the Champs Elysées is for television journalists, well-heeled tourists and other *arrivistes.* First-class managers seek out first-class dining at the conservative Lucas-Carton, Taillevent, Sormani and a few other restaurants. Even power breakfasts are catching on in Paris. Today, the movers and shakers congregate at the Hotel George V restaurant, where 350 francs will get you a cup of coffee and a croissant delivered with whispered service in formal dress. The regulars are addressed by name in hushed tones.

Easing everyday pressure

The relaxation of tension at lunch is the reverse side of exaggerated stress and strain in the office environment. An official office meeting with a senior manager would be brisk, organized and punctual. One Paris CEO I know is famous for setting the alarm on his digital wristwatch for 30 minutes at the start of a typical meeting. At the 'beep-beep', he leaps from his leather chair in mid-sentence, declares the meeting terminated, and escorts the visitor to the door. But in a three-star restaurant he struggles to relax as he pinches breadcrumbs from the tablecloth and repeatedly straightens the cutlery. Through clenched teeth, he talks of his *très bourgeoise* private life.

At a typical business lunch, conversation will jump to the menu, to the wretched quality of French television, to a recent movie, an appreciation of each dish as it arrives, to the wine, and when things get really warmed up, to the family. Meanwhile, each person keeps a discreet eye on the other's choice of food, table manners, wine expertise and interaction with the waiter and wine steward. All these details are clues to one's appropriateness as a dining companion – and, by extension, as a business associate.

When the friendly phase is over, both parties suddenly assume upright posture and explain the business they wish to accomplish. The change of mood is unmistakable and will surprise a beginner. The first time it happened to me, I felt I had gone backwards in a time warp – back to the bad old formal relationship of an hour earlier, the pre-lunch era.

Restaurant staff make it their business to recognize and coddle their big spenders from the business-lunch world. One of my regular dining partners had a weakness for white truffles, a delicacy so expensive it is unknown to most of us. Throughout our lunches the *maître d'hôtel* nipped in and out of our space with his silver truffle mill every ten minutes, offering more and more. Each turn of the crank interrupted the business conversation with a non-threatening food comment, creating pleasant cycles that prevented the table talk from ever getting too heavy or too deep.

The ultimate business luncher is he who maintains an account at the restaurant so that the sordid subject of coin never arises. When the allotted time has elapsed, the host and guest calmly arise and depart as the staff bows and scrapes. He seems to own the place.

The wine – it's a long story

The cultural contrast is clearest when the wine is tasted. Most French will not be satisfied to say to the wine steward, '*C'est bon*', and resume normal conversation. They will want to express an opinion, display their erudition, or very rarely, send back the bottle with a flick of the wrist and a wrinkling of the nose. Foreigners are on thin ice here, and can pick up some bad habits. One American journalist enjoyed the power of tasting so much he once sent back a bottle of Evian mineral water. The waiter, professional to the end, obeyed without batting an eye.

I once heard a French colleague discourse for five minutes on why a certain red wine was *coquin* (impish, rascally). In fact I brought this on myself. I had asked him to explain the use of *coquin* in the wine context, not quite believing his choice of words. Of course he was miles ahead of me. Not only did he know why he used the term, he cared. Holding his glass up to the light, his elucidation went approximately like this:

'We have here an unpretentious red that seems to wash harmlessly over the palate, leaving a mild sensation of fruity dryness with a hint of mother earth. We swallow, and we say good-bye. Then a second later, the rascal sneaks back up to the palate and grabs your tastebuds with a jolt you can't believe. And watch out for that kick. What a playful little devil!'[1] Eventually we returned to the business at hand, but the relationship was transformed. I felt I had been admitted to the secret club.

Fortunately I had the presence of mind not to repeat an expression that had landed me in trouble a few years earlier in Paris during one of my first visits. Sipping too much Bordeaux rouge at a Paris dinner party in the 16th *arrondissement*, I quoted my brother-in-law's favourite wine compliment: '*C'est comme si la Vierge Marie m'avait pissé dans le gosier*'. ('It's as if the Virgin Mary peed down my throat.') That was enough to send the hostess bolting for the kitchen, murmuring, '*Ce n'est pas joli. Ce n'est pas joli.*'

I was not invited back.

Two hours four minutes of tabletalk

The restaurant appears here to stay as the venue of choice for business relationships to flourish. 'One of the best ways for the French to get to know clients and business associates is to meet away from the office in pleasant surroundings, and lunch and dinner serve this purpose well,' writes the master of cross-cultural clashes, Edward T. Hall, in his book *Understanding Cultural Differences.* He quotes a study that shows the average French business lunch lasts two hours and four minutes, compared to one hour and seven minutes in the United States. Business dinners may last several hours. This seems excessive? Hall's advice is, in effect, when in France, do as the French do. I found lunch to be one of the easier peculiarities to grow accustomed to.

It would be wrong, however, to expect the French lunch to be all pleasure or quickly assimilated. More often than not, I found the ritual to be so demanding as to destroy the potential satisfaction. Every meal was like having lunch with a head-hunter, each movement scrutinized for signs of a possible personality disorder. To the discerning observer, adding salt before tasting your *entrecôte* can raise questions – you may be impulsive, indiscriminate or maybe even adventurous.

In the finest restaurants of France it takes very little to make the eyebrows dance. A few incidents come to mind:

---

1 A sophisticated American, on the other hand, might have expressed it thus: 'Hmmm . . . Nice aftertaste. Fill 'er up.'

— AND MAKE THAT BEEF
VERY WELL-DONE.

Mysterious culinary rules

- At a three-star establishment in central Paris I once heard a *maître d'hôtel* openly gasp when an American guest, having spent ten minutes puzzling out the menu, announced, 'Nope. No starter for me.' I expected the cook to come charging out of the kitchen demanding to know why not, but he let it pass.

- A New York sophisticate was taken down a notch when the *patron* refused to carry out his request for a well-done steak. 'Not in my establishment,' he said. 'I knew he was going to say that,' the visitor murmured, sliding low in his seat. He took it rare and forced it down.

- On another occasion half a dozen kitchen staff peered anxiously through the doorway as the waiter asked my table why one guest had failed to clean up his plate. 'Sorry, it was only jet-lag' was accepted as a reasonable explanation.

For those unaccustomed to wine at lunch the experience can be a problem. Although trendy Frenchmen are beginning to forgo wine in the presence of foreigners, it happens only rarely. You are expected to partake and to express your judgement. To keep sober, you can fake consumption by taking bird-like sips every few bites. Others round the table can be counted upon to make up for your abstemiousness.

Eating has its place, and it is a very large place, in the French business ritual. With preparation, with effort, and with some discreet advice from friendly natives, the determined foreigner can carry off the business lunch. When you are accepted at the captain's table, you have arrived.

10 Words: The Subtlest Weapon

'What is called the art of speaking is eminently the
talent of the French, and it is by the art of speaking
that one rules over men.'

Theodore Zeldin

'Language disguises thought. So much so, that from
the outward form of the clothing it is impossible to infer
the form of the thought beneath it . . .'

Ludwig Wittgenstein

The language barrier for the foreigner working abroad is frequently
underestimated, and the struggle against this barrier is a lonely one. But if
international business develops as expected, more and more managers will
be crossing borders to work in strange cultures and unfamiliar languages.
Many managers will suffer for the privilege, for a giant obstacle awaiting
them is the all-important game of competitive communication. Mastering
the art of speech where you work is essential to survival. Only the fittest
can compete in the war of words – the arena where management problems
are identified, defined and resolved.

Among foreigners working in Paris, linguistic skills cover the full
spectrum, from total ignorance to silver-tongued fluency inherited from a
French mother or father. The fluency claimed on CVs, however, is often
a meaningless concept until tested in a closed native environment.

Language problems can be such a potent ego-destroyer that many
people find it difficult to speak frankly about the limits of their own
fluency. Even the speaker cannot know the depth of his or her linguistic
knowledge without plunging into the ultimate stress test, being there
alone. The problems of foreign-language communication simply cannot be
appreciated otherwise. Even then, only the foreigner knows how much
trouble he is having. Only the foreigner knows that he is forced to think
twice as fast merely to avoid losing ground.

Learning by degrees

Linguists will tell you that humans communicate on varying levels of
complexity. Foreign-language fluency of the first degree is what you learn

at university: 'The sky is blue.' 'The pen of my aunt is on the table.' Beyond that, as fluency progresses, words begin to transform themselves into a powerful weapon, an instrument of domination supercharged with suggestions, references, ideas, deliberate obscurity and (depending on the objective) seduction, foreboding or innuendo. The speaker may want to display his own intellect, he may want to amuse, or, least likely of all, he may simply want to communicate. In competitive situations, he will use language skills to bluff, intimidate or confuse his adversary. It is the rare foreigner who can win on this terrain.

In France, pride of language makes the challenge greater than in many other countries. Foreigners are expected to appreciate the *finesse* of good French and to respect the great past that the language has accumulated. Even today the French squirm at any reminder that their linguistic domination was lost to the English in 1919. To be precise, English achieved equal status with French in diplomacy at the Versailles Peace Conference, when for the first time in international affairs French-only proceedings were considered inadequate. English was added as an alternative and equally acceptable working language. Again at the end of World War II, French was nearly brushed aside by the Americans and the Russians. Peace treaty documents were written first in English and Russian. Only cries of protest led to the French language being restored as an additional version, and the French had to fight yet again when at the creation of the United Nations only three working languages were proposed – English, Spanish and Russian. In fact, the threat to French predated these incidents. English had been gaining steadily on French leadership as the language of commerce since the mid-nineteenth century.

Playing with fire

The French language is neither dead nor dying, however. Novelists and semanticists play with it like fire. The late academic and critic Roland Barthes liked to write in the stratosphere: 'I am but the imaginary contemporary of my own present.' Raymond Queneau wrote a novel in low-life slang, leading off with the now-famous telescoped word, '*Doukipudonktan?*' ('Where's that funny smell coming from?') His classic *Exercices de style* took a 109-word paragraph and rewrote it in 98 stylistic variations including: kitchen Latin, the sonnet, in words of two to five letters in length, haiku poetry, gastronomic and medical. He published it in

1947 and the French still love it and quote from it today.

Street children mangle it and spit out new forms of words and sentences that are incomprehensible to foreigners, for example *verlan* (backward-formation of words, including the word for the form itself, which comes from reversing *à l'envers,* which means backward), an old wordgame that has become part of current slang.

Among themselves, the educated French like to exchange oblique verbal volleys across the office, estimating each remark as a 'second-degree' or 'third-degree' allusion, or the truly obscure and the ultimate compliment, a 'tenth-degree' remark. I knew I had made progress when I could make second-degree comebacks to some of the smart repartee.

Like the culture it reflects, French can be an impressive tool in the hands of a master. The great Francophile and chronicler of France, Theodore Zeldin, goes so far as to say that a Frenchman of the nineteenth century could be recognized not by his appearance but 'by the way he used language, the way he thought, the way he argued'. The same applies today.

The French are eager to discuss ideas, a challenge for many US and British managers even in their native language. Abstractions do not come naturally to the Anglo-Saxons, but the French are taught from a young age to argue concepts in the most elegant terms. For a foreigner to keep pace, he must understand that they like to start at the beginning of a problem, to advance from the simple to the complex, or from the general to the specific, the way Descartes would have liked to hear them talk. This grates on the nerves of a heart-of-the-matter Anglo-Saxon, who wants to jump straight to the point, to talk business efficiently. A Belgian friend is also impatient with the time-wasting and often vacuous French style that is beautified for the sake of being beautiful. 'I am exasperated by the way they love to substitute style for substance,' he told me. 'Why can't they cut out the excess verbiage?'

Working as a journalist in France can be painful when a Cartesian-trained interview subject, pondering a simple question, leans back, examines the ceiling tiles, and says, 'Ah . . . For that, we must consider the origins of the problem.' He may not reach the twentieth century for another 45 minutes, by which time the interview is over.

A popular book on the French Social Security system is written in the same vein. It opens with a long-winded and largely irrelevant discussion of welfare in Rome, Sparta and Athens. On occasion, when the substance is there, the structure can be useful. I once conducted a one-hour interview with the writer and editor Jean-Jacques Servan-Schreiber that consisted of two questions: 'How's it going?' and something like 'Could you explain that please?' His argumentation was so beautifully structured, so lucid, that it could have been published with hardly a change. As interviewer, I was unnecessary. He answered more questions than I could ever have thought up. Before publishing the interview, I reworked the text with him to insert ten intelligent-sounding questions.

Linguistic stress

To the non-native speaker in the office, language pressure leads quickly to operational problems. The trouble starts on the mechanical level, remembering the simplest things. I found myself on guard for such problems as these.

- **Memory**. The memory seems to work at about half its usual efficiency because familiar references and connections are squirrelled away somewhere else in the brain – in English. French references for most newcomers have not built up enough girth to qualify for their own 'port', or connection, in the brain. The most important events of the day, happening in French, will often vanish from the memory as if they had not happened at all.

- **Names**. Even getting to know the staff presents unexpected difficulties. Names tend to be unfamiliar and to sound the same, Pascal and Pascale, Jean-Pierre and Jean-Philippe, Bernard and Bertrand, Yannick and Annick.

- **Faceless audio**. A ringing telephone on the desk can cause abdominal spasms. The newcomer secretly wonders, 'Will I seem incompetent if I ask the caller to repeat?' A stream of words down the phone line, without body language to aid comprehension, can be intimidating; nothing is sweeter at the end of a day than a surprise phone call in one's native tongue.

Ignorance of the linguistic challenge among people, including French people, who have never faced the language barrier is sometimes hard to believe. A shop owner in Dieppe, a major fishing port just across the English Channel from Britain, once complimented me after a brief chat for speaking four languages.

'Four?' I asked.

'Yes,' she replied. 'You said you speak French, Russian, English and American.'

When I explained that English and American were the same language, she blushed and roared with laughter.

'Ooo la-la, I have learned something new today,' she said.

Starting over

The newcomer to France needs about a year to relearn the French he thought he spoke. As he gets into the stride of a language, he naturally gains confidence and takes risks with slang and new expressions. And as his mastery grows, so does his nerve. Suddenly, linguistic trapdoors seem to fly open. After falling into a dozen or so of them in the first few weeks, one wants to make a defensive retreat, and question whether it ever made sense to try to fence with the natives in their own language. Embarrassment at mismatched verb endings, errors of gender or simple slips of the tongue will be a daily occurrence. Memories of them return like ghosts in the middle of the night. A colleague took me aside early in my tenure to inform me I had just bid farewell to a woman who was leaving on holiday by saying I 'desired' her. I had wanted to say I envied her. (I should have said, '*Je vous envie*'. Not, '*J'ai envie de vous*'.) The gaffe nagged at me for months.

Fortunately it was not with her, but with another colleague, that I tried out my newest textbook slang over a working lunch by observing that he was not '*dans son assiette*', a common expression meaning 'in good form' but literally translated as 'in his plate'. After he burst out laughing, I realized that this is not an expression to be used at the table when people are in front of their dinner plates. But I had some private satisfaction an hour later when he finished eating, pushed back his chair, and to show off *his* textbook English, said, 'I'm fed up'.

The non-native speaker in listening mode ends up groping for the general meaning, much like a lip-reader, rather than worrying about every word coming at him. The flood of words and meaning can be over-whelming,

MONSIEUR N'EST PAS
DANS SON ASSIETTE... ?

Linguistic false friends

especially at the end of a full workday. The brain simply says 'uncle' after too many words.

Ego interference

I once had a German boss whose poor linguistic skills gained him a reputation for *non sequitur*, which got more bizarre as the day wore on and his brain lagged increasingly behind the conversation. Never one to show his vulnerability, he sheltered his ego by ignoring questions and diverting the conversation. Anything rather than being seen to fumble with his English. His colleagues went along with his surreal zigzags to spare him humiliation.

No school can prepare a student, not even a German, to function at full capacity in a foreign language. Even a mixed marriage, the so-called sleeping dictionary, is of limited use. The vocabulary is all wrong. Kitchen French, much less bedroom French, is of little use in a budget meeting. George Bernard Shaw cast doubt on the whole second-language effort with this sweeping dictum: 'No man fully capable of his own language ever masters another'.

One problem is that French vocabulary, the basic building block, is in constant evolution. Despite the efforts of the Académie Française, French is as mobile as English or any other living language.[1] The French today have reduced their language to its roots, half out of irony, half out of impatience. They don't even say *café* for coffee shop. Now it's *caf*. Breakfast is not *petit déjeuner,* but *petit déj*. Restaurant is *resto*. A note from your secretary might say you had a *perso* telephone call for an *RV* (rendez-vous). And each speciality has its lingo. Some of the jargon of the publishing business is representative. In everyday speech, *'conf'* is shorthand for *conférence*; *'doc'* stands for *documentation*; *'rédac'* for *rédaction*; *'techno'* for *technologique*; *'actu'* for *actualité*; *'édito'* for *éditorial*; *'dia'* for *diapositive* (colour slide); *'modif'* for *modification*; and *'réal'* for *réalisation*, *'fab'* for *fabrication*. The heavy dose of mathematics and science in French education made for a shorthand business lingo, such as a 'delta' for variable, '>' for 'greater than' and '<' for 'less than'; a 'beta-test' for a dry run; an 'n' for 'example'. Reliable mental arithmetic is expected of everyone. Pure Latin pops up everywhere: *'recto'*, *'verso'*, *'primo'*, *'secundo'*, *'tertio'*, *'a priori'*, *'a posteriori'*.

Out-talking the adversary

Spurning perfectly good French vocabulary, the switched-on French manager will pepper his speech with English words, spoken as French

---

1 In 1991, the Académie Française decreed a short list of newly permissible variations on the language. A couple of accents were dropped, and one or two hyphens were eliminated from compound words such as weekend. The newspapers went berserk.

words, such as *'outsider'*, *'brainstorming'*, *'peanuts'*, *'turn-over'*, *'best of'*, *'basic'*, *'private joke'*, *'full-up'* and *'fair play'*. English and French can be mixed and matched to the point that colleagues lose track of the meaning and have to grovel for an explanation, thus giving the speaker one point in his game of one-upmanship.

Now a new category of pidgin English is developing: vogue words from English that are grammatically frenchified, complete with accents and conjugated endings. A busy manager is no longer simply *'occupé'*, he is *'overbooké'*, or even *'squeezé'*. To redesign a publication is to *'relook'* it. A handsomely conceived new product is *'très design'*. Two pieces of anything that do not go well together are *'un misfit'*. When you have left the hotel, you have *'check-outé'*.

Even in more conventional terms, the language is loaded with vocabulary pitfalls – apparent cognates that turn out to be false friends. I was stunned when, shortly after my arrival, a French colleague cautioned me against acting like a *démagogue*. But she confessed that she was a bit *lunatique*. In both cases, nothing could be further from the truth. I was a listener, a persuader, a consensus person. Demagogues were men who ruled by harangue. Not so in French, a language I had spent 25 years studying. In French, a demagogue manager is a person who seeks to be loved by his staff – a cardinal sin in French management. I was being warned against getting too chummy with my subordinates. As for her being *lunatique*, she was only saying she became moody under pressure. Lunatic in English originally had the same meaning – changing moods with changing phases of the moon.[2]

Why they have the edge

The interloper gradually realizes that native speakers will always benefit from an edge in business dealings. In all walks of life this advantage is abused. Waiters do it, shopkeepers do it. Civil servants and government bureaucrats do it. Sometimes without intending harm, employees will do it to their foreign bosses.

My most Kafkaesque experience in France was not in the office but in the Préfecture de Police. I was obliged to obtain residence papers from the

---

2 My demagogue status now established, I became aware of an even graver problem. I was being told to get serious about erecting hierarchical barriers between myself and my staff.

French bureaucracy. Entry to the foreigners' chamber at the Versailles Préfecture is guarded by three or four young men and women who sit on a platform and bark instructions in rapid, slangy French to the foreigners who come humbly seeking workpapers. Some foreigners manage to grasp the general sense of the instructions and move on to the proper window for the next humiliation. Those who don't, and ask for clarification, are laughed at or scolded as the gatekeepers chuckle among themselves. The African worker ahead of me in the queue never had a chance.

'Oh-la, this one can't speak French properly,' the young lady official said loudly to her colleague as the African stood before her stammering his question.

Finally the hapless worker wandered off in search of a familiar face in the crowded hall. Obviously he had suffered before.

Although I was trussed up in a silk necktie and smart suit, they wanted nothing to do with me, either. I lost half a day's work, and was told to return in two months for more of the same. Next time I brought my French wife with me, and the clerk ended the confrontation with her in a staring contest, finally backing down. I was granted a one-year work permit.

Grappling for control

At the office, the foreign manager must expect great additional pressure in his day-to-day work as he struggles to maintain a semblance of authority while assimilating higher and higher levels of language. He will have to work doubly hard at achieving the right substance presented in the correct form.

At the beginning, every spoken sentence is a test. Even in small talk, employees will probe for weakness, to test the boundaries of his comprehension, and find ways to use the linguistic advantage. Reading the morning post becomes a challenge. Paperwork piles up with alarming speed as linguistic overload turns to linguistic mayday. Writing a memo requires total concentration, sometimes more than one can muster. Fielding telephone calls can leave the manager in a sweat. Face-to-face meetings with subordinates on delicate subjects such as attitude or performance are a true test of the foreign manager's nerves.

My German ex-boss, who came to London a few years ago over-confident of his heavily accented English, managed to stumble in his first sentence while addressing his new staff. Attempting to put his people at ease with a touch of German levity, he said with a reassuring chuckle, 'I am the kind of manager who likes to choke'. Twenty-five nervous employees reached for their throats.

Although not unintelligent, he also had trouble keeping names of his staff straight. Nearing linguistic mayday late one afternoon, he congratulated the wrong man on a promotion and salary increase. Another day, he invited the wrong man to lunch, and had to spend two hours thinking of something to say – in English. He returned to Germany after six months, and ran the division from a distance. Everyone was relieved.

Always testing

Most employees will do the foreigner no favours. More likely, they will continually test his comprehension in subtle ways, using language as a weapon. Some employees will fire sideways comments at meetings in a slang that only a native could pick up. It is then up to the manager to decide whether to show his vulnerability by asking for an explanation, by guessing at what is happening, or by simply rising above the rudeness.

No preparation will be sufficient to allow the foreigner to keep pace with the locals in corridor chitchat or in business meetings. No accent acquired through language study will be sufficient to allow the foreigner to blend into the linguistic culture and thus be trusted as a mother-tongue speaker would be. The only solution for the accent is to start the language before puberty and stick with it. If you didn't have that good luck, it is probably too late. Most mature British or American vocal cords cannot grapple successfully with the gutturals of German, the uvular 'r's of French, the yerihs of Russian, or the throat disease that is called Dutch.

The foreign manager's accent, however slight, makes it difficult for the French to use the '*tu*' form of address, meaning 'you' in the familiar, friendly, trusting sense. The '*vous*' in this case is used for two intertwined purposes: it indicates respect for authority, but it also holds the overly friendly manager at arm's length.

The *tu/vous* problem causes awkwardness among the French as well. A new employee in a company will not be sure at the outset whether to be familiar or not with his colleagues, his bosses, and others farther up and down the chain of command. His solution is to construct sentences carefully without personal pronouns. When cornered, he can still take refuge in the third person. As a last resort he can say to his boss, '*Est-ce qu'on veut que je travaille de cette façon?'* ('Does one wish me to work in this way?')

One Frenchman who works for Britain's Japanese-owned computer company ICL told me how he had learned to turn the tables on the English-speakers. Making a virtue of necessity, he flaunts his incompetence in the language when attending management meetings in London. His English is so rudimentary, he says, that he dispenses with protocol, formulas of *politesse* and all euphemisms.

'I deliver my message in a few direct words,' he says. 'People don't like me, but they understand me. I don't care. I can say unpleasant things in a few seconds. It saves everybody a lot of time.'

Sweet revenge

That Frenchman is lucky to be so arrogant. He gets pleasure from speaking English poorly. He is perhaps taking sweet revenge for a lifetime on the receiving end of bad French, or no French at all, from his British colleagues.

The same underlying bitterness emerged in a study of the negotiators who set up the Channel Tunnel project. The French said their British counterparts seemed to consider themselves superior to the rest of Europe. 'It is always up to *us* to make an effort, especially as far as language is concerned,' said one of the members of the French team. 'Even if they can speak French, they will speak English, without making any concessions for the fact that we are foreigners.'[3]

Understandably, the French are frustrated by the acceptance of English and, since East European liberation, German as the languages of international business. The result is the absence of French in executive suites around the world. An intellectual I knew in Paris likes to say on his gloomier days that English is rolling into Europe at such a pace that French will be a dead language in two more generations. An alarmist view, no doubt, but the government seems nearly as pessimistic. To reverse the slide, the Elysée Palace holds annual summit meetings of the heads of the 35 francophone nations to encourage the development of the language. It has had no noticeable effect.

---

3 Study by Inter-Cultural Management, Paris.

The francophone countries want to construct an 'alternative to the Anglo-Saxon model of the universe'. Why they want to do this is not clear. Inside France, however, the objective is more rational: to avoid a tribal family of languages in which businessmen would speak English, intellectuals would speak classic French, immigrant workers bastard French, and ordinary people television French.

The solution is to keep French pure. Even this effort does not pass without irony. Its chief promoter in the mid-1990s was government minister Jacques Toubon, known to French and English alike as Jack Allgood. Toubon's aim was not to conquer English, he only wanted to make it as fashionable to speak French as it is to speak English.

To the French business person, however, language is no joke. The arrogance of the Anglo-Saxon business community is a daily humiliation for any Frenchman trying to operate on an international scale. Even in Paris, foreign businessmen will often try to get by with speaking English to their French counterparts. A recent poll showed that 31% of American multinationals consider that foreign language proficiency is unnecessary for their managers heading abroad. Only 20% of those surveyed require overseas managers to speak the language of their adopted country. The other 49% had mixed feelings.

English required

In France today, some of the more forward-looking international companies have capitulated, making it policy to speak the lingua franca of international business. Alcatel NV and Cap Gemini Sogeti both attempt to conduct their international meetings in English. Such is the pressure to expedite business, however, that they sometimes lapse into French. A German manager at Alcatel tells of finding himself in a meeting of a dozen French colleagues. Although he spoke no French, the language was French, leaving him out. A few highlights were translated as the meeting went on.

The question remains, should a foreigner attempt to keep up with the talented French, or will it always be a losing battle? The answer is yes, keep trying, keep improving. In time, the anxiety eases, and colleagues will eventually be pleasantly surprised at your progress. Some of them might even tell you so.

11 The Crooked Road Forward

'If one can read only French, it is difficult to know
much about what the rest of the world is thinking. That
is why France retains its character, and its sense of being
a self-sustaining unit.'
                                                Théodore Zeldin

'An equidistant perspective can take many forms.
However managers do it, however they get there, building
a value system that emphasizes seeing and thinking globally
is the bottom-line price of admission to today's borderless
economy.'
                                                Kenichi Ohmae

'Nationalism is a cheap instinct and a dangerous tool.
Take away from any country what it owes to other countries,
and then be proud of it if you can.'
                                                John Fowles

As I had hoped and expected, working at close quarters within a foreign culture greatly illuminates one's understanding of human behaviour. New patterns of life, new values, new frictions are discovered and must be dealt with in real time. A humdrum daily existence is quickly transformed into state of constant alert. For the unprepared, the new environment can be difficult to face. For the devoted internationalist, it is a welcome stimulant. The personal satisfaction of day-to-day successes can be of a high order. The day I survived my first staff meeting, arguing in French and winning a few points, was a private triumph.

I often think how fortunate I was to escape the American Midwest, where I might have ended up selling ploughs and seed corn to the local farmers. I would surely be brain dead by now. My language study, begun at university, opened new worlds that would not have been accessible otherwise. By the 1980s, the Anglo-Saxon business world was beginning to understand that learning to think and behave as an internationalist would be the next path to success.

It was a lucky coincidence – for this was just what I wanted to do with my life. The concept of the global economy took shape in the following years, satisfying this wanderlust in me and in thousands of professionals around the world. What we were looking for was something more than the 'armchair anthropology' experienced by diplomats and foreign journalists who live in a closed circuit of briefings and cocktail parties for fellow foreigners. And we wanted more than a life in Britain, which scarcely presents a challenge for any native English speaker. France opened these doors to me.

Business gurus make a good living off two debates these days: 'change management' and 'going global'. Among the internationalists, you will find ideas on these themes converging and conflicting, some of them insightful, some seriously misguided. Among those I chose to ignore is the advice that there is an easy way to adjust to a new culture. One professor urges us to concentrate on the 'cultural universals' (the common denominators, the similarities that unite all societies), and all will be fine. He obviously has not tried managing firsthand away from home.

The true way is the gradualist approach towards integration. Although strong leadership is required it must not turn to brute force, which nearly always breeds resistance. I was determined to persuade my people to follow me voluntarily. I wanted to reshape the work culture into a kinder, gentler image based on the desire to produce results together. It had worked before in New York and in London; it was working elsewhere in the world. According to all the business schools and management thinkers, it was the enlightened way towards the goal of humane management. It was a way of taking the warfare out of professional life.

It did not work in France. I now know that the implications of modern management techniques can be upsetting to cultures that are deeply entrenched. The variety of barriers examined in this book help explain the problem. Concepts of individuality, lack of trust, rejection of teamwork all play their role in France. The overriding barrier to professional mobility is the self-perpetuating French *élite*. This system has created a caste of men and a few women who are conditioned to take and hold power as a divine right, much like the aristocracy of the past. Layered on top of these barriers is a welfare system that makes people problems cumbersome and costly to solve – often more trouble than they are worth. And as any manager knows, the right mix of talented people is the secret of producing the best results.

In my company as in others, the determination to protect the status quo also helps explain the resistance to change that French society is wrestling with today. The French have learned to live with the tall pyramid structure in society and in business. The 'haves' intend to 'keep', and the have-nots seem to know their place. But the true barriers to change have their roots in the mechanics of how change actually happens. The different views in Latin countries and the Anglo-Saxon cultures are at opposite ends of the spectrum. Latins want change to be programmed and controlled – and they are expected to resist. The Anglo-Saxons watch change happen almost randomly, whenever it needs to happen, and will bend with it like reeds in the wind.

The younger generations will surely find a world increasingly more hospitable to the internationalist. Lower barriers to trade are already encouraging cross-border business. The managers who understand the markets they are moving into will integrate more quickly with the culture and economy they plan to serve.

Lower barriers will also inevitably extinguish some of Europe's quainter business and cultural corners – perhaps even some of France's seemingly arbitrary management practices. Andrew Wilson, a former executive at McDonnell Douglas Corp., makes the analogy between the global economy and the world's oceans. Although oceans cover 60% of the planet, only 10% of the world's animal species live there. The explanation, says Wilson, is that the strongest predators rule in the wide-open waters of the ocean. There is no place to hide; there are no barriers. Something like this Darwinian scenario may be the pattern in the twenty-first century. Economic fitness, and therefore survival, will come from dealing successfully in that 'ocean' of markets outside your home culture. Eat or be eaten.

The slow process of convergence has been under way since the European Union's Treaty of Rome in 1957. The global economy in the past ten years or so has broadened and accelerated the process. Tastes in some standard products have already converged, we are told by marketing people, achieving new economies of scale. The trend and its eventual payoff will work its way down the price ladder to the consumer.

But this battle is far from over. Some consumers stubbornly cling to their cultural programming and resist global homogenization. In France, roadsigns are sprouting up in the countryside saying: 'France: love her or leave her'.

What I saw in France left me in little doubt that the process will be slow and painful. Difficult adaptations face all the Europeans in their single market, perhaps a single currency at some point in the distant future, and perhaps a single political federation in the twenty-first century. On an even grander scale, the convergence of global markets is a well-documented trend. Our children and grandchildren will undergo more and more of these cultural adjustments. We may as well show them the way.

Now that I have looked in detail at the workplace in France, the best I can say is that change might come eventually, but only a minority of companies – those with international interests – seem willing to give these ideas a try today. The prognosis is no better in some other markets. In my 20 years in Europe, the gap separating countries has remained dismayingly wide. France, like Britain, like Germany, like Denmark, suffers from what Aldous Huxley called national multiple-personality disorders. The young tend towards integration, but the over-40s cling to the symbols of national identity. No one can say whether today's young people will feel the same when they grow older or whether they will become inward-looking like their parents. And other groups – nationalists, small businesses, opportunists of all types – will drag their heels for their own reasons. As long as mature generations resist change, it will be wrong to say, as some have, that Europe is on the move against the nation-state.

Contentment in fragmentation looks more likely to be tomorrow's reality. The great majority of Europeans simply cannot relate amicably to their neighbours. In simple terms, a foreign accent is almost always an insurmountable barrier to close relationships, business or personal.

At the same time, like all the world's industrial economies, France is feeling the pressure to change, to open its borders and to become more competitive on a global scale. The old protectionist practices that shielded French business from the outside world for so long must gradually be adjusted to the realities of international competition. This was the admirable motivation behind the decision of my managing director to bring me into the company. She had a Columbia University MBA, and she knew that France could not persist in its isolation. Yet at the individual level, we found that the barriers are still formidable.

Nevertheless, convergence of tastes and, to some degree, harmonization of cultures, seems predestined. in the long term. These changes will come as a byproduct of close collaboration, and collaboration with neighbouring countries will be Europe's key to achieving the single market objectives of a coherent trading zone with 400 million consumers. Cross-cultural contact, and the closer the better, is the cornerstone of this *rapprochement*. With time, tolerance and preparation, the future cross-cultural workers have a better chance.

To improve their prospects of enjoying the experience, these ten points will be useful to keep in mind.

1. **Temperament**. Determine whether you actually have an internationalist's temperament. A good test is to recall how many foreigners you have spoken with over the past month. The past two months? If you have the stretch to recall, or if you can admit the number is zero, you may be heading abroad for the wrong reasons.

2. **Environment**. In considering any offer for a cross-cultural business experience, stick to companies that already have an international team at the management level. Try to avoid being the pioneer, only non-PCN (non-parent-company national). Like organ transplants, foreign bodies risk being rejected. Management teams that have a good mix of nationalities already in place will have prepared the way for new ideas and styles. The company culture will by definition be more receptive to foreign influence. The barriers to change will already have been battered down.

3. **Ethics**. Check the company's and the country's fundamental outlook on ethics before you sign that contract. Nothing will cause discomfort like a basic ethical conflict. If you are an accountant heading for Italy, make sure you can live with Italy's triple book-keeping system – one set for the shareholders, one set for the tax inspector, and one accurate set for yourself.

4. **Realism**. Do what you can to ensure that the company is realistic about its international ambitions. In the quest for instant international credentials, there is a lot of self-deception about – companies seeking global gratification in the short term. The euphoria quickly fades away, however, leaving a sense of disappointment. Quick forays into international business or international management techniques can be difficult for the parent company to absorb.

5. **Compensation**. Negotiate a safe employment package. It will be expensive, and the receiving company should accept this fact. An international career means running your life in two countries at once. Financial interests, family, maintenance of your home culture all incur costs. Demand a safety net, an exit clause, a parachute, to protect yourself against the worst case.

6. **Family**. Make sure your family is in tune with your choice. Your own stressful adjustment (acculturation) will be enough to handle without worrying about disorientated teenaged children, an isolated wife and a household to manage where nothing is familiar. Do you all speak the right languages?

7. **Humility**. Make it clear to your new staff that you understand how different you are. Ask for indulgence and flexibility. Demonstrate yours, and hope the two will meet somewhere down the line.

8. **Language**. Master the language. Carry the burden of cultural and linguistic adjustment openly. If you also want *them* to change, try to introduce the change in their language, and move gradually towards your objectives.

9. **Commitment**. Take on the challenge with a long time horizon. The adjustment process might consume two years. Only then will you start to show business results.

10. **Breadth and depth**. Ask yourself whether you are interested in the country's history and culture. If you are, you will be better equipped to ride out some of the worst moments of the first two years. Everything that happens will be of at least academic interest. If the country and its people leave you indifferent, this may not be the place for you.

The French say they want to be leaders in the development of Europe. The enthusiastic talk is no doubt sincere, but the gap between the idea and the reality is still large. Major multinationals excepted, it is the perception, not the reality, of going international that appeals to them. Lip service will continue to be paid generously. But getting there will often prove too much to handle.

I was repeatedly asked by my director of human resources to slow down. 'Remember, you are in France. We have our way of doing things.'

Appendix
Inaugural Speeches

How to Seduce a Progressive French Staff

An all-purpose inaugural address by a newly arrived foreign manager who wants to establish rapport with his staff. He appeals to reason. He persuades through sensitive explanation.

You may wonder: what am I doing here?

I feel privileged to be among you today. This is the beginning of an association that I hope will be long and fruitful. You represent a proud company with a culture all its own, and I look forward to getting to know how it works.

Let me begin by acknowledging that I am the foreigner here. I am different. I look different. I'm sorry, but I will never be like you. Yet I am here because our top management has decided that I have something of value to contribute to our common effort. I bring new ideas that I hope will stimulate you and help you think in fresh, exciting ways.

I am here also because I am interested in your country and in your culture. I want to learn from you. I like your attitude towards life. I like your educational system. Your history. I like your sense of humour.

I am here to explore with you and to find a better way to work, based on our different experiences. We have many things to teach each other. We will both have surprises ahead of us. But in good faith, we will be pooling our knowledge of the world to make this a better place to work.

We *must* pool our knowledge to stay globally competitive. Isolation and protectionism are self-defeating attitudes. Gutless attitudes. Doomed attitudes. The way ahead will call for courage. Yes, we may expect the process to hold some surprises, but what is life without surprises? It is bound to be more interesting than an isolated national context. There will even be times when it will be amusing.

Our international effort will work because it will prepare us for the international business world that is just beginning to happen. We may consider that we are part of a new trend towards the globalization of management.

What problems can we foresee? Nothing we can't handle together. First, we must learn to accept our differences as normal and natural. Second, we must maintain a healthy curiosity about ideas from the outside. Third, we must learn to look forward to change.

The phenomenon of change in business has been studied thoroughly and competently by the business gurus. We know what it is all about. We are not re-inventing the wheel here. Change is not a threat – it is normal and should be welcomed. Progress and improvement can come only from a process of change. Those who want the status quo forever are condemned to be the odd men out.

But I am asking you to accept a double dosage: change from a foreign source. Together we will do better than the experts predict. They say that people in a new international situation must return to infancy and learn every little thing over again. This will not be the case if we accept that we are all in the same boat – all rowing in the same direction. But we can handle our problems better if we anticipate them.

I propose that the basis of our relationship be the simple concept of honest work – our best work. From this will flow a new force of loyalty in both directions. I will ask you in return only to assume the responsibility of applying your talents to the fullest. I certainly intend to. You will gain greater satisfaction as you give your best efforts to create solutions. How can this be anything but a positive turning in your life?

This is a workplace where we want to find professional satisfaction. Good work is not you-against-me, or us-against-them or me-against-you. We all want this company to survive and prosper, for as *it* does, *we* will.

Thank you for hearing me out. I will be happy to take your questions.

Taking Charge of a Traditional French Company

An inaugural address by a newly arrived manager who wants his French staff to understand who is boss and what he expects of them. He assumes the role of the all-powerful, all-knowing boss. He expects obedience.

What I am doing here

I have been in town a week and it's about time we got a few things straight, men. I hope to stay a while, so you had better get used to me. Your way of working leaves something to be desired, but don't worry – I can already see what needs to be fixed.

Let me begin by reminding you that I come from another country, so naturally we will have our differences. You look different from me, you act differently, and you don't speak my language. You will never be like me. But my boss has chosen me for this job, because I have a reputation for knowing how to change things. I know how to get the job done. Bear with me a while, and you will pick up my methods.

I know you are aware of what has been going on in management thinking in my country. I want you to learn from it. Try to put it in the context of my country's history, educational system, and our terrific sense of humour.

I am here to help you find a way to be more productive, more proactive, and that real bottom line, more profitable. You have a lot to learn, but I am sure you can do it. Let's be frank – you will have to do it, or else. Listen, pay attention, and you will soon see that this will be a better place to work for all of us.

You *must* adapt to new ways of working in order to stay globally competitive. Staying wrapped up in your isolated protectionism will be the death of you. These are gutless attitudes. Doomed attitudes. Stupid attitudes. The way ahead will call for courage – the courage to accept surprises good and bad. But this will be interesting. Anything would be more interesting than just staying at home to milk your local market, right?

I am going to teach you how to operate outside the boundaries of your usual territory because that's what the rest of the world is doing. You see, we are going to play with the big guys, swim with the sharks. You'll love it.

Will we have problems? You bet we will. But we will sort them out in a hurry. First, as I said before, you and I are different, so you will have to accept that. Second, be ready for the ideas from outside that I will be installing. Third, I am going to change things, so don't be surprised.

The business gurus know what the process of change entails, and anyone who has been in business has heard it all. There is nothing new under the sun. Let's face it: change is something we have to get used to. How else are we going to make any progress? It is time for us to get moving or we will be stuck forever with the status quo.

Today I am telling you to prepare yourselves for a double dosage. You are going to get change, and you will get it from a foreigner. The experts say that people in international situations must return to infancy and learn every little thing over again. Let's not believe that kind of thing. The good news is that children learn fast. I am sure you will find a way to keep up with me. We are all in the same boat, and I do not intend to name it the Titanic. (Laughs.)

The thing that will make this relationship work is the simple idea that you have to trust me. It might take a while, but it will come naturally after a bit. You know, like they used to say in Watergate, your hearts and minds will follow. Once you trust me, I want you to be loyal to me. Fiercely loyal. Work hard, do your best, and you will find that our relationship really is a positive thing.

After all, what we want from our little deal here is to raise productivity. It's in all our interests. It's not a you-against-me situation. That won't wash. As this new relationship starts to work, we will all benefit. The company will prosper, and you will get to keep your jobs.

Thanks for listening. Now get back to work.

Bibliography

— (1987) *French–British Negotiation. A Cross-Cultural Comparison*, Paris, Inter Cultural Management.

Appignanesi, Lisa (editor) (1989) *Ideas from France: The Legacy of French Theory*, London: Free Association Books.

Ardagh, John (1990) *France Today*, London: Penguin Books.

D'Assailly, Gisele, and Baudry, Jean (1977) *Le Savoir-Vive*, Paris: Marabout.

Barsoux, Jean-Louis, and Lawrence, Peter (1990). *Management in France*, London: Cassell Education.

Birrien, Jean-Yvon (1990) *Histoire de l'informatique*, Paris: Presses Universitaires de France.

Blum, Jerome, *et al.* (1966) *The Emergence of the European World*, New York: Little, Brown & Co.

Bootzin, R.R., Bower, G.H., Zajonc, R.B., Hall, E. (1986) *Psychology Today*, New York: Random House.

Braudel, Fernand (1988) *The Identity of France*, Volume 1, New York: Harper & Row.

Calder, Nigel (1986) *The English Channel*, London: Chatto & Windus.

Camber Porter, Melinda (1986) *Through Parisian Eyes. Reflections on Contemporary French Arts and Culture*, Oxford: Oxford University Press.

Chanlat, J.F. (editor) Amado, Gilles, Faucheux, Claude, Laurent, Andre (1990) *L'Individu dans l'Organisation: les Dimensions Oubliées*, Quebec City: Presses de l'Université Laval, Collection Sciences de l'Administration.

Clerc, Christine (1982) *Le bonheur d'être Français*, Paris: Grasset.

Collett, Peter (1993) *Foreign Bodies: A Guide to European Mannerisms*, London: Simon & Schuster.

Corder, Colin (1992) *Some of my Best Friends are French*, London, Hitchin, England: Shelf Publishing.

Daninos, Pierre (1954) *Les Carnets du Major Thompson*, Paris: Hachette.

Daudy, Philippe (1991) *Les Anglais*, London: Headline.

Deal, Terrence, and Kennedy, Allen (1982) *The Rites and Rituals of Corporate Life*, New York: Addison-Wesley.

Delbanco, Nicholas (1989) *Running in Place: Scenes from the South of France*, New York: Atlantic Monthly Press.

Drucker, Peter (1989) *The New Realities*, London: Heinemann.

Druon, Maurice (1964) *Le pouvoir, notes et maximes*, Paris: Hachette.

Fowles, John (1981) *The Aristos*, London: Triad Grafton.

Gaillard, Jean-Michel (1987) *Tu seras président, mon fils*, Paris: Editions Ramsay.

Giscard d'Estaing, Valery (1988) *Le pouvoir et la vie*, Paris: Compagnie 12.

De Gramont, Sanche (1970) *The French, Portrait of a People*, London: Hodder and Stoughton.

Hall, David L. (1982) *Eros and Irony*, Albany: State University of New York Press.

Hall, Edward T. (1983) *The Dance of Life: The Other Dimension of Time*, New York: Anchor Books/Doubleday.

Hall, Edward T., and Reed, Mildred (1990) *Understanding Cultural Differences*, Yarmouth, Maine (USA): Intercultural Press.

Hofstede, Geert (1991) *Cultures and Organizations. Software of the Mind*, Maidenhead, England: McGraw-Hill.

Johnson, Paul (1983) *A History of the Modern World: From 1917 to the 1980s*, London: Weidenfeld and Nicolson.

Levi, Primo (1986) *The Drowned and the Saved*, New York: Summit Books (Simon & Schuster)

Maurois, André (1960), *A History of France*, New York: Grove Press.

Mermet, Gérard (1991) *Euroscopie*, Paris: Larousse.

Mermet, Gérard (1992) *Francoscopie*, Paris: Larousse.

Moran, Robert, *et al.* (1993) *Developing the Global Organization*, Houston: Gulf Publishing.

Moss Kanter, Rosabeth (1983) *The Change Masters. Innovation for Productivity in the American Corporation*, New York: Simon & Schuster.

Mitchell de Quillacq, Leslie (1992) *Power Brokers: An Insider's View of the French Financial* Elite, New York: Lafferty Publications.

Ohmae, Kenichi (1990) *The Borderless World*, New York: Harper Business.

De Panafieu, Alexandra (1990) *Les superstitions populaires*, Paris: Jacques Grancher.

Peyrefitte, Alain (1976) *Le mal français*, Paris: Plon.

Pickles, Dorothy (1965) *The Fifth French Republic*, London: Methuen.

Platt, Polly (1994) *French or Foe?*, Paris: Culture Crossings.

Plesis, Alain (1987) *The Rise & Fall of the Second Empire 1852-1871*, Cambridge: Cambridge University Press.

Poniatowski, Michel (1975) *Conduire le changement*, Paris: Fayard.

Queneau, Raymond (1947) *Exercices de style*, Paris: Gallimard.

Szarka, Jay (1992) *Business in France. An Introduction to the Economic and Social Context*, London: Pitman.

Taylor, Sally Adamson (1990) *Culture Shock! France*, Singapore: Times Books International.

Voltaire, *The Philosophy of History*, Chapter 7.

Vovelle, Michel (editor) (1988) *L'Etat de la France pendant la Revolution 1789–1799*, Paris: Editions la Découverte.

Winchester, Hilary P.M. (1993) *Contemporary France*, London: Longman.

Zeldin, Theodore (1980) *France 1848–1945, Taste and Corruption*, Oxford: Oxford University Press.

Zeldin, Theodore (1980) *France 1848–1945, Intellect and Pride*, London: Oxford University Press.

Zeldin, Theodore (1988) *The French*, London: Collins Harvill.

Index